A USER'S GUIDE TO NEGLECTFUL PARENTING

GUY DELISLE

TRANSLATION BY HELGE DASCHER

Also by Guy Delisle:
Jerusalem: Chronicles from the Holy City
Burma Chronicles
Pyongyang: A Journey in North Korea
Shenzhen: A Travelogue from China
Albert & the Others
Aline & the Others

Translated by Helge Dascher. With special thanks to Rob Aspinall, Dag Dascher, Mark Lang, and Julia Pohl-Miranda.

www.guydelisle.com
www.drawnandquarterly.com

First paperback edition: June 2013
ISBN 978-1-77046-117-8
Printed in Canada.
10 9 8 7 6 5 4 3 2 1

Library and Archives Canada Cataloguing in Publication:
Delisle, Guy
    A User's Guide to Neglectful Parenting / Guy Delisle.
ISBN 978-1-77046-117-8
    1. Graphic novels. 2. Fatherhood—Comic books, strips, etc.
3. Parenting—Comic books, strips, etc. I. Title.
HQ756.D445 2013   306.874'2   C2012-907121-8

Drawn & Quarterly acknowledges the financial contribution of the Government of Canada through the Canada Book Fund, the Canada Council for the Arts, and the National translation program for book publishing for our publishing activities and for support of this edition.

This work, published as part of grant programs for publication (Acquisition of Rights and Translation), received support from the French Ministry of Foreign and European Affairs and from the Institut français. Cet ouvrage, publié dans le cadre du Programme d'Aide à la Publication (Cession de droits et Traduction), a bénéficié du soutien du Ministère des Affaires étrangères et européennes et de l'Institu français.

Liberté • Égalité • Fraternité
RÉPUBLIQUE FRANÇAISE

-The Tooth

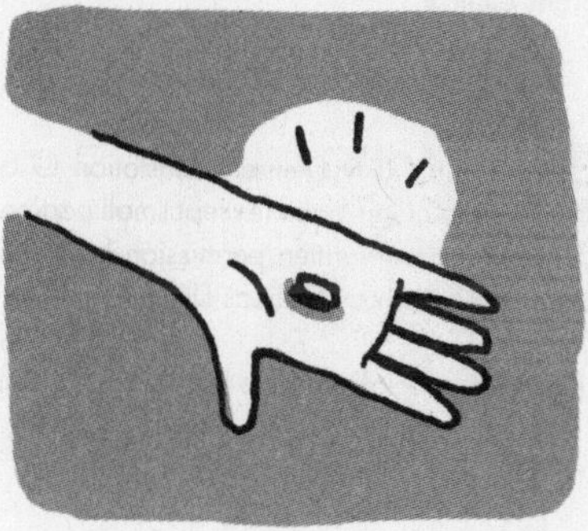

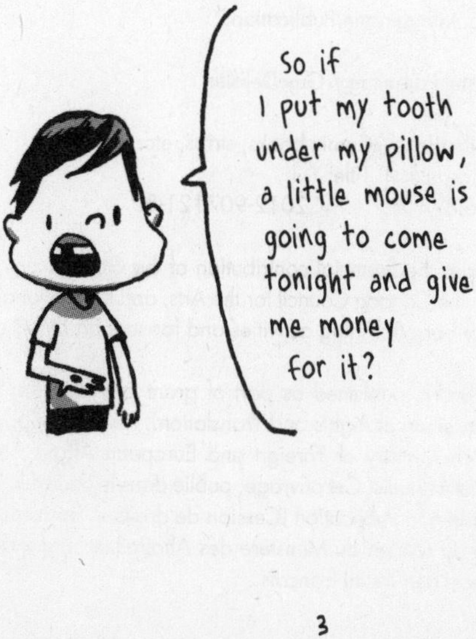
So if I put my tooth under my pillow, a little mouse is going to come tonight and give me money for it?

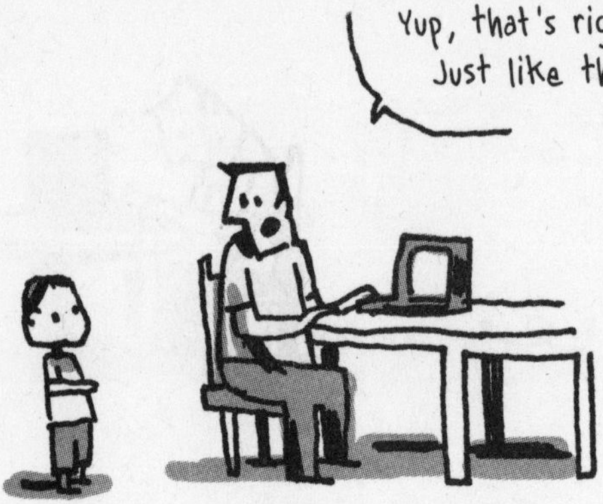
Yup, that's right.
Just like that.

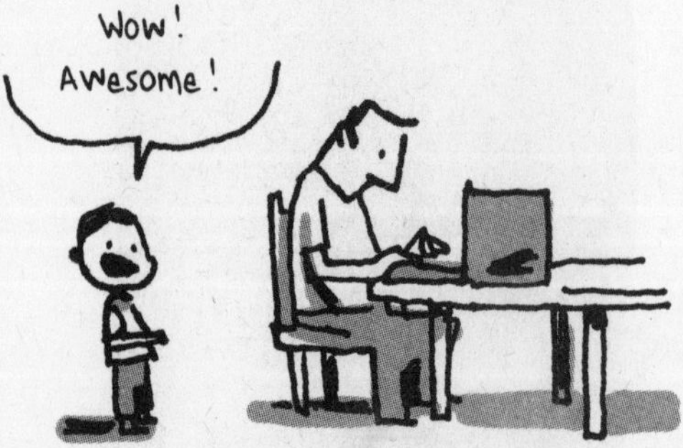
Wow!
Awesome!

That
Evening

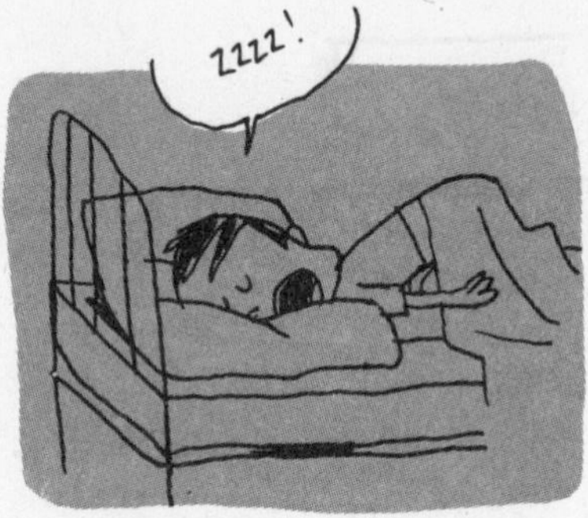
ZZZZ!

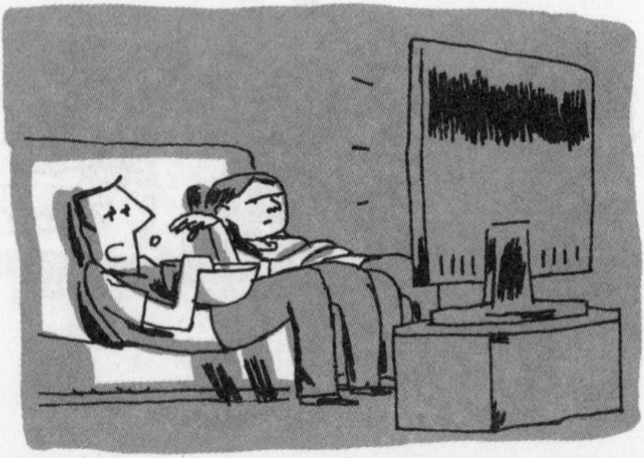

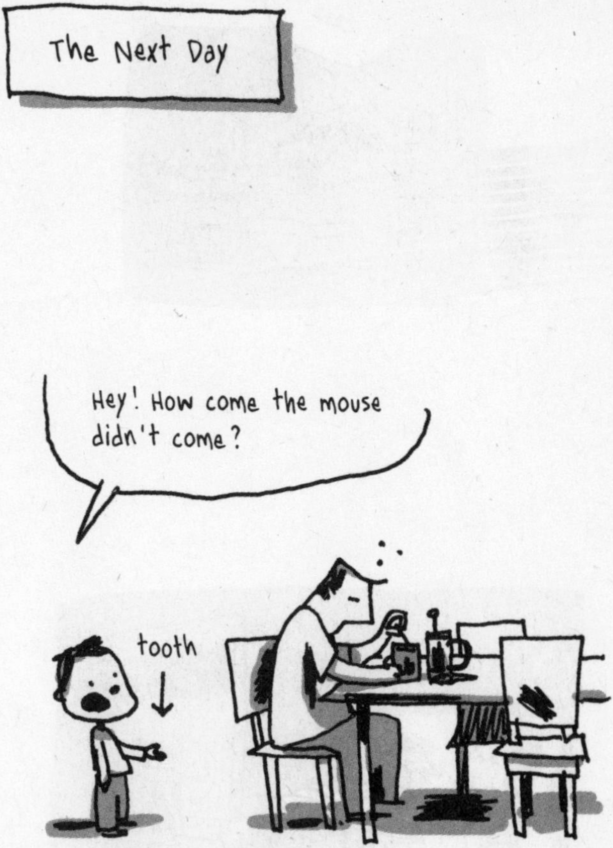
The Next Day
Hey! How come the mouse didn't come?
tooth

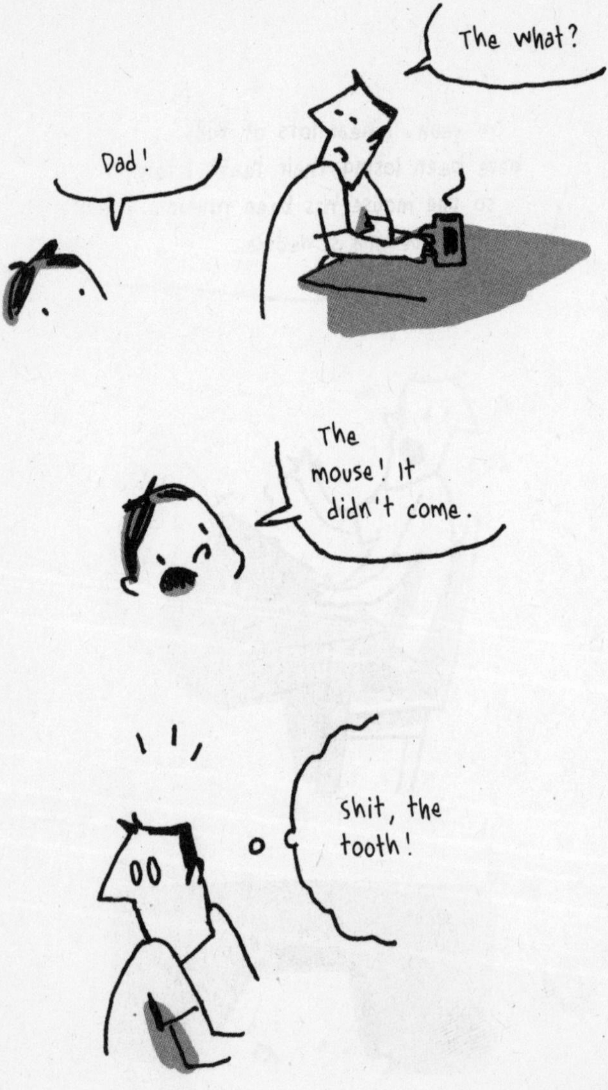
Dad!
The what?
The mouse! It didn't come.
Shit, the tooth!

Oh yeah. I hear lots of kids have been losing their teeth lately, so the mouse has been running behind schedule.

What a drag, huh?

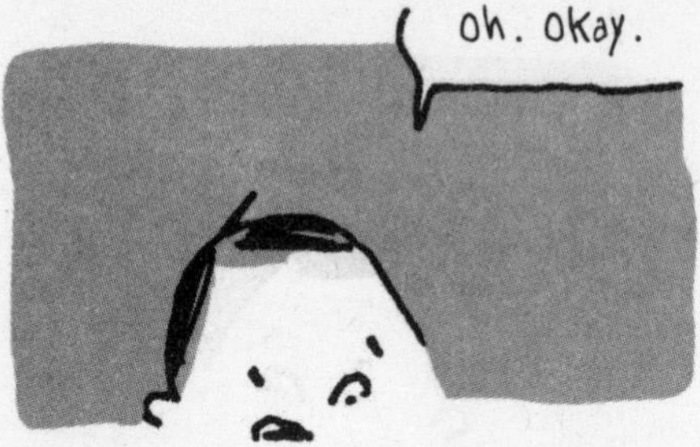
Oh. Okay.

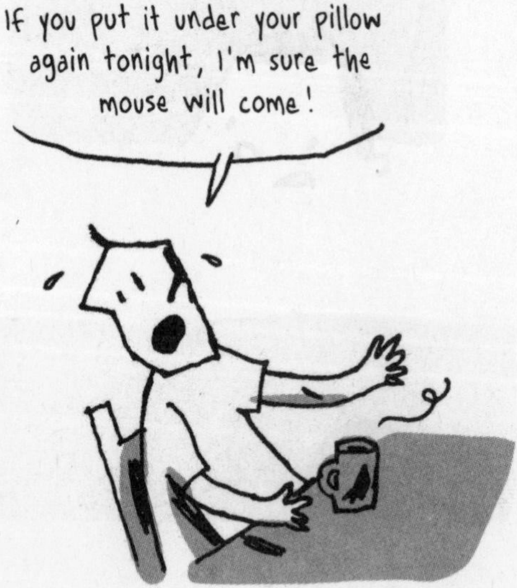
If you put it under your pillow again tonight, I'm sure the mouse will come!

cool!

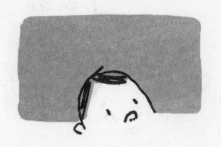

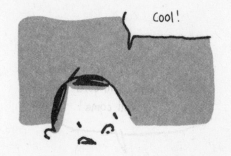

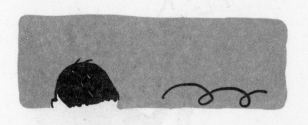

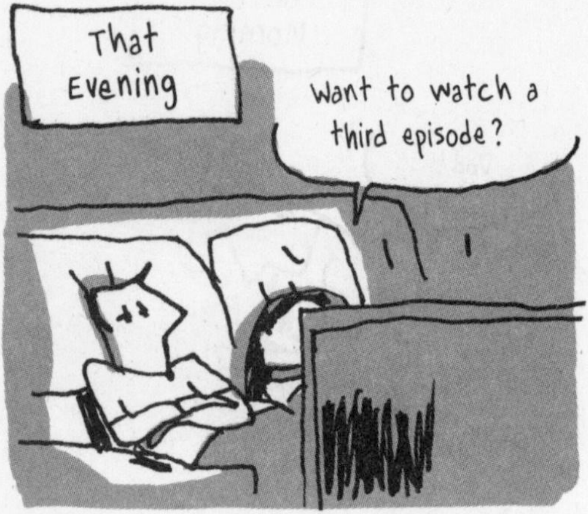
That Evening
Want to watch a third episode?

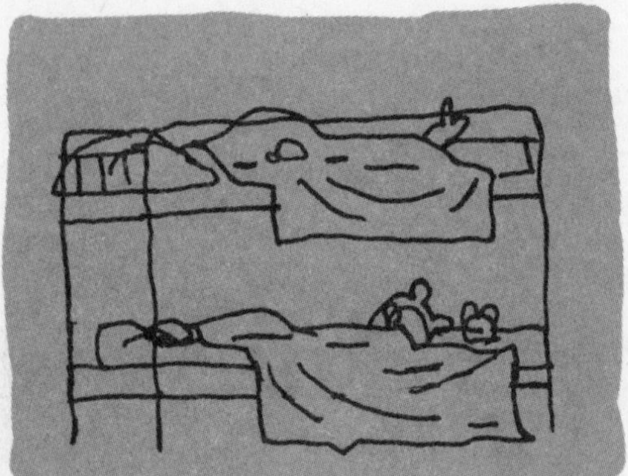

The Next Morning
Dad!

The mouse still hasn't come!

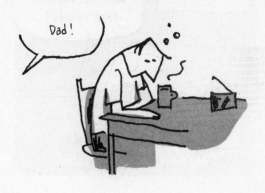

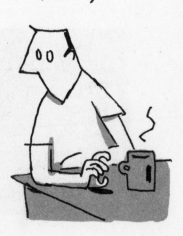

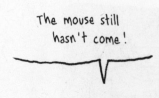

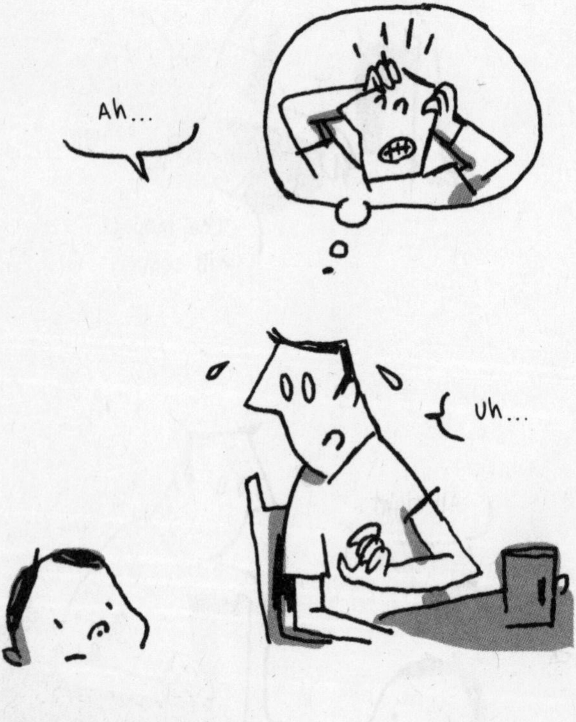
Ah...
Uh...

Don't worry about it. Sometimes it takes a few tries before it works...

I'm sure it'll be fine tonight.

The mouse will come.

All right.

That
Evening

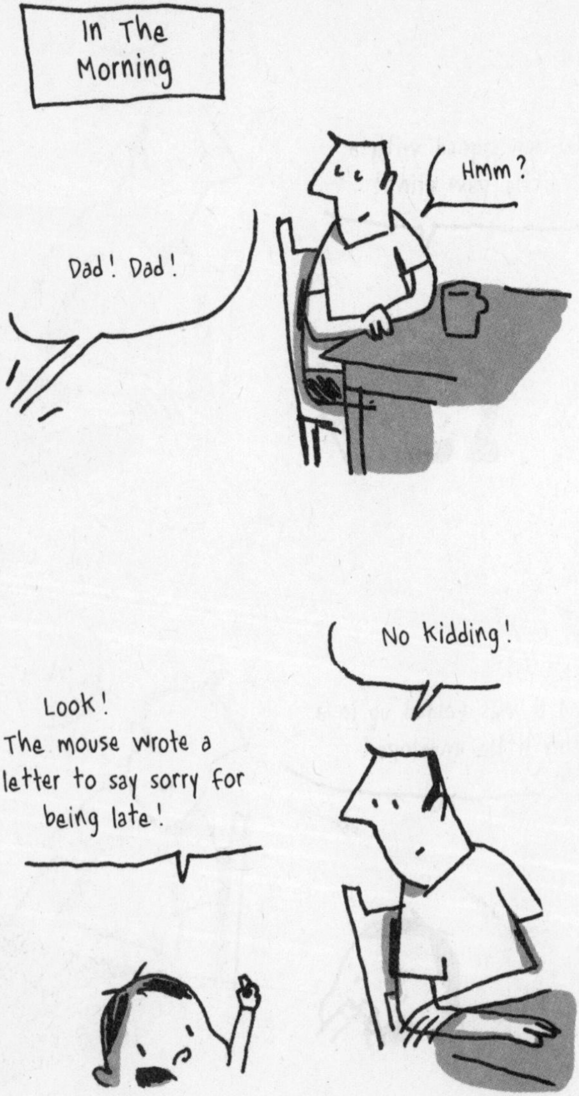
In The Morning
Dad! Dad!
Hmm?
Look! The mouse wrote a letter to say sorry for being late!
No kidding!

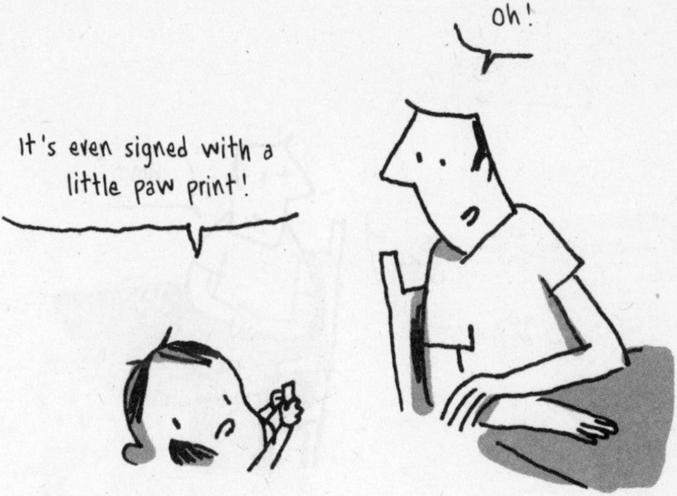
Oh!
It's even signed with a little paw print!

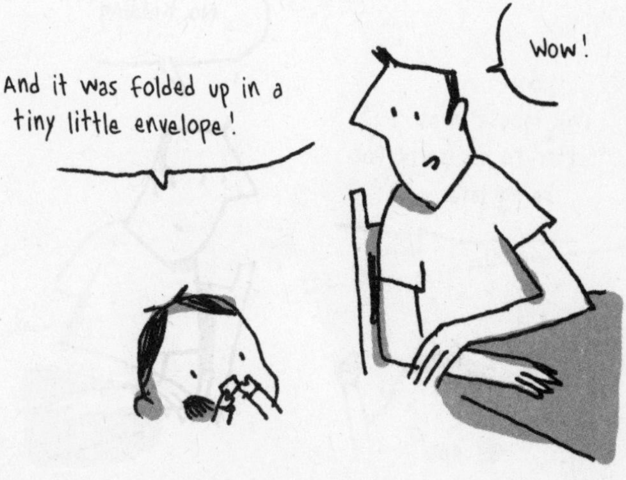
And it was folded up in a tiny little envelope!
Wow!

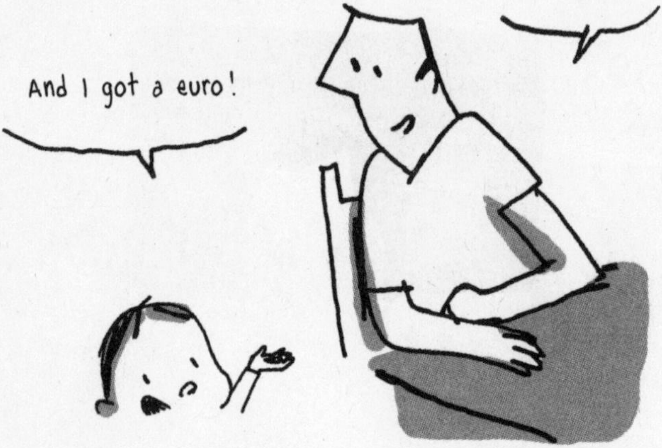
And I got a euro!
Nice!

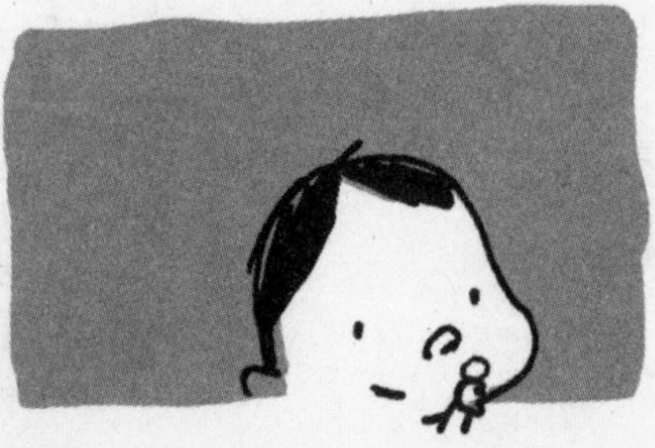

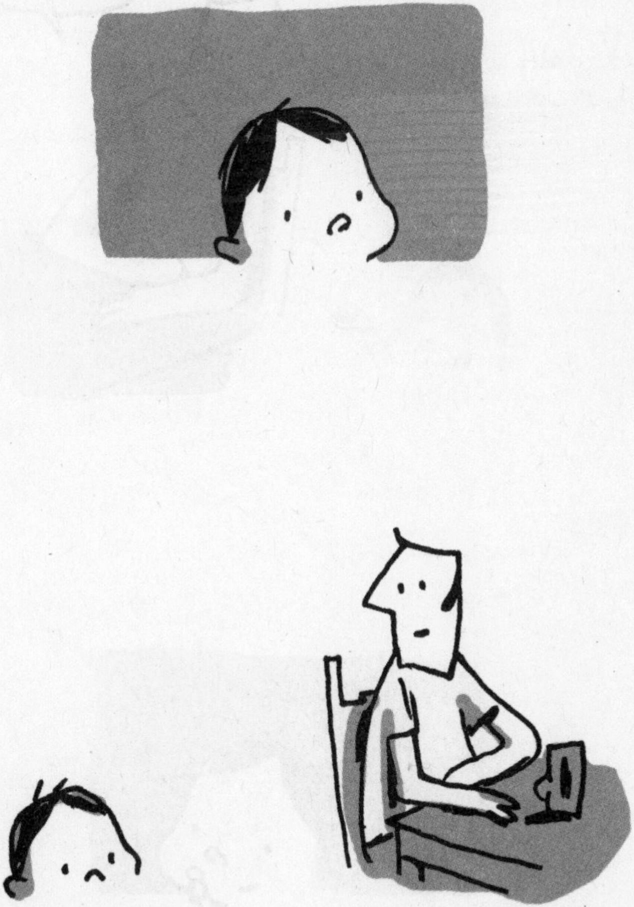

Hey Dad, it's not you and Mom who leave the money while we're sleeping, is it?

Are you kidding...

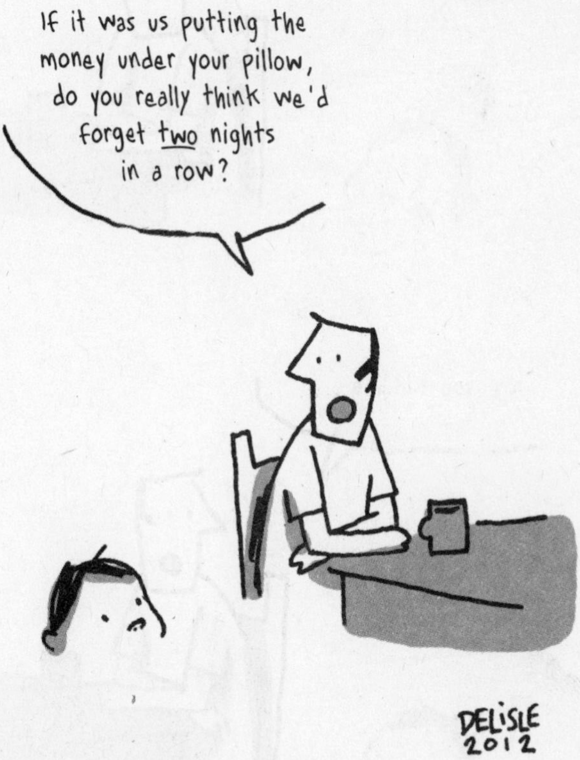
If it was us putting the money under your pillow, do you really think we'd forget two nights in a row?
DELISLE 2012

-The Apricot

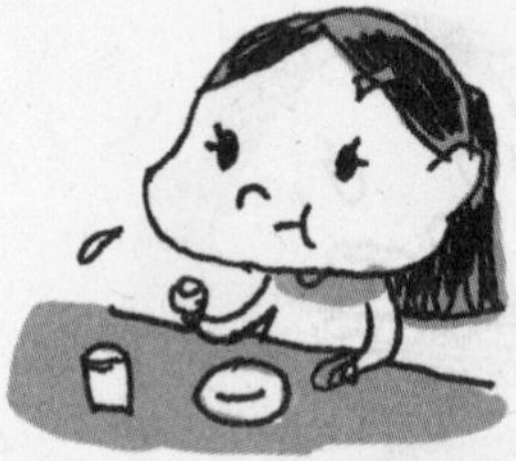

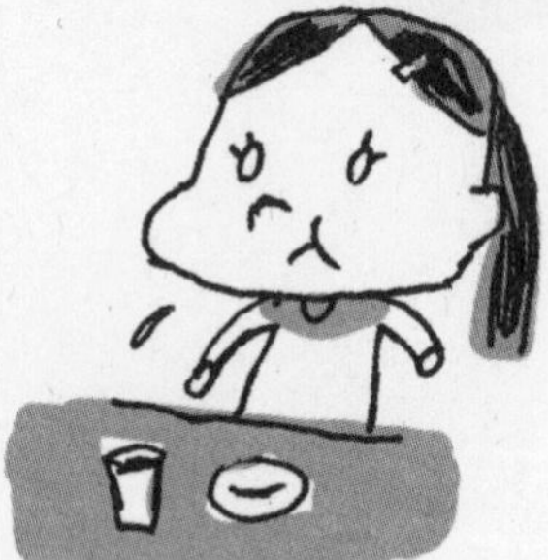

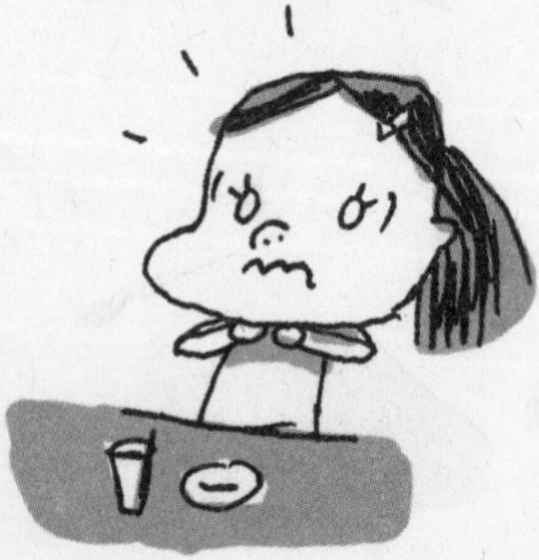

Dad!

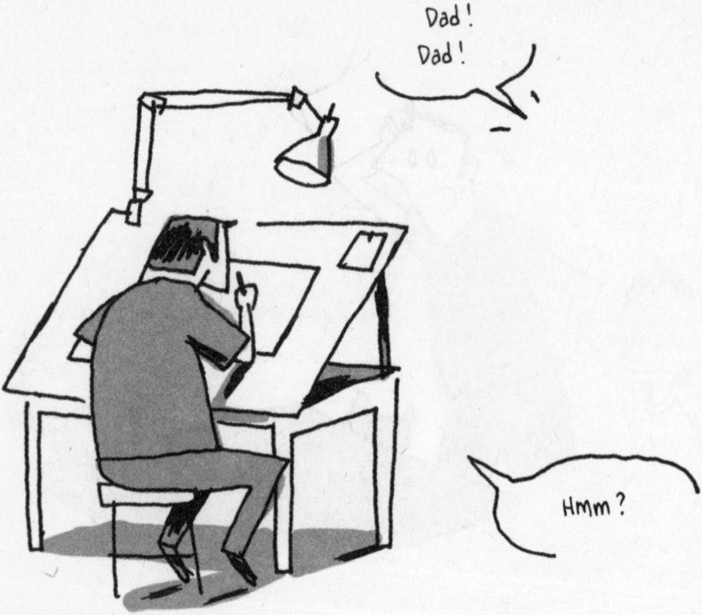
Dad!
Dad!
Hmm?

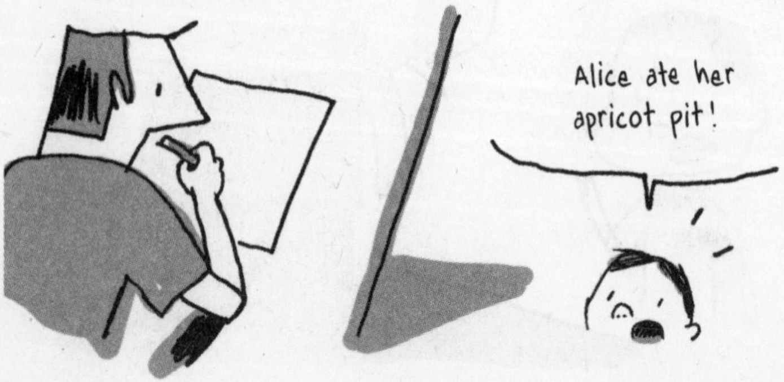
Alice ate her apricot pit!

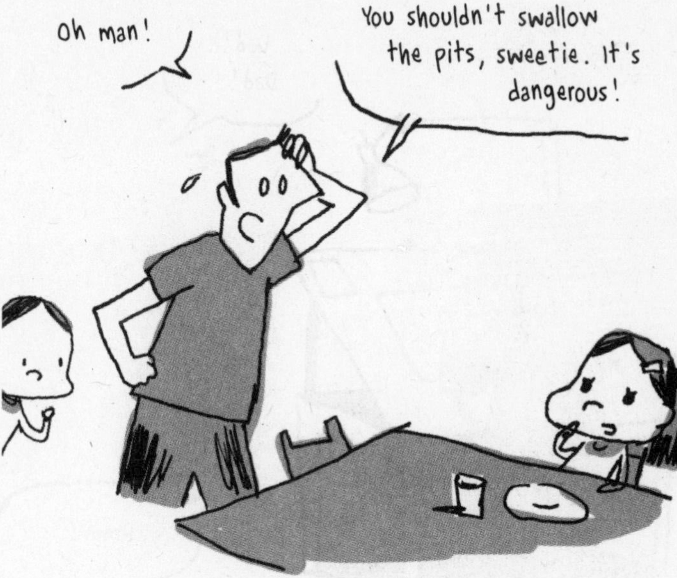
Oh man!
You shouldn't swallow the pits, sweetie. It's dangerous!

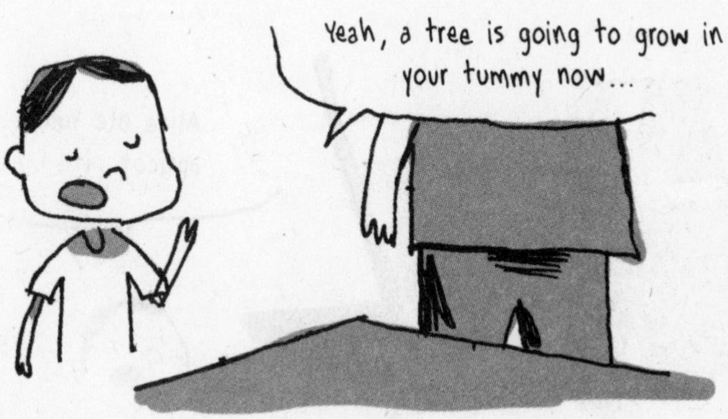
Yeah, a tree is going to grow in your tummy now...

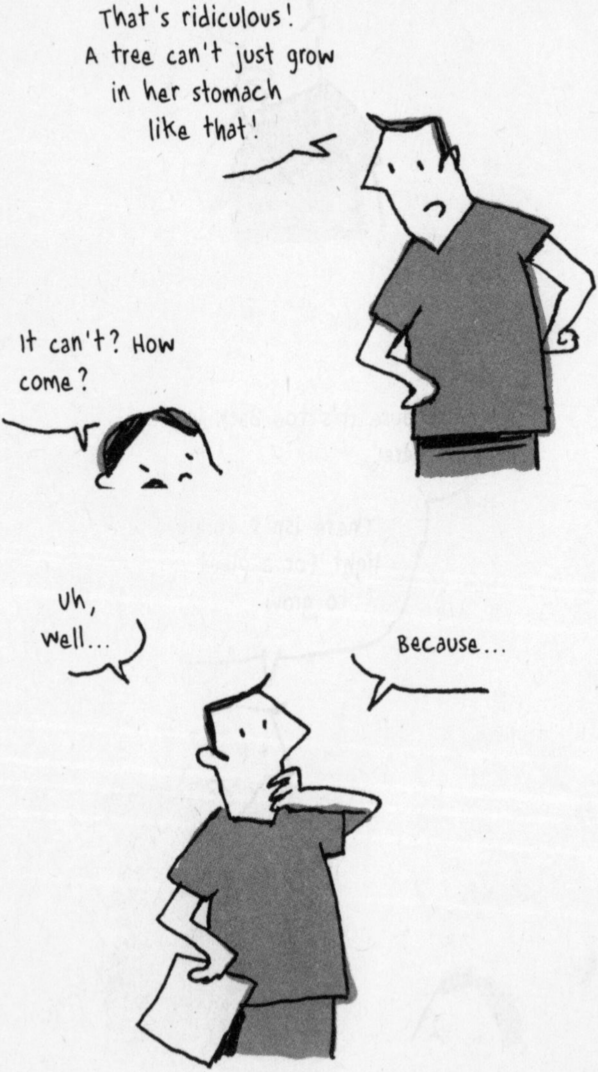
That's ridiculous! A tree can't just grow in her stomach like that!
It can't? How come?
Uh, well...
Because...

Because it's too dark in there.

There isn't enough light for a plant to grow.

But if Alice keeps her mouth open long enough, I guess it could sprout.

So you better not sing anymore.

If I were
to draw it,
it would look
something like
this.

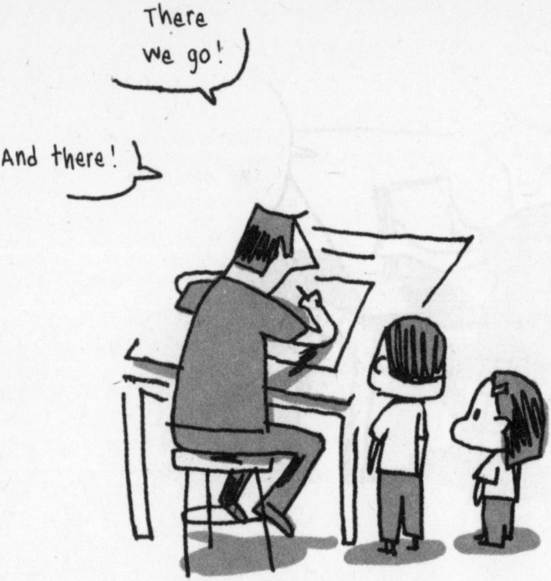
There we go!
And there!

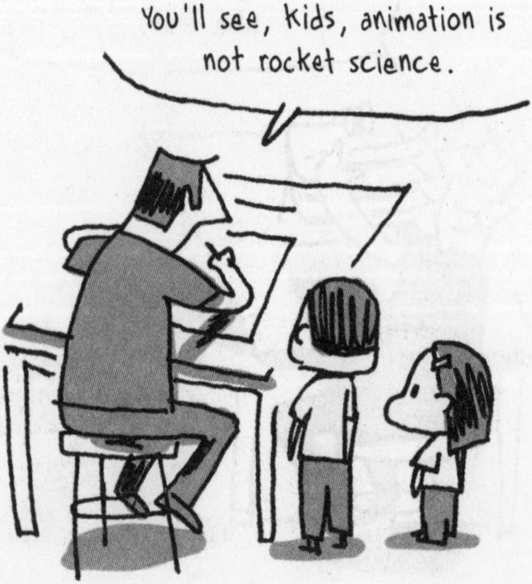
You'll see, kids, animation is not rocket science.

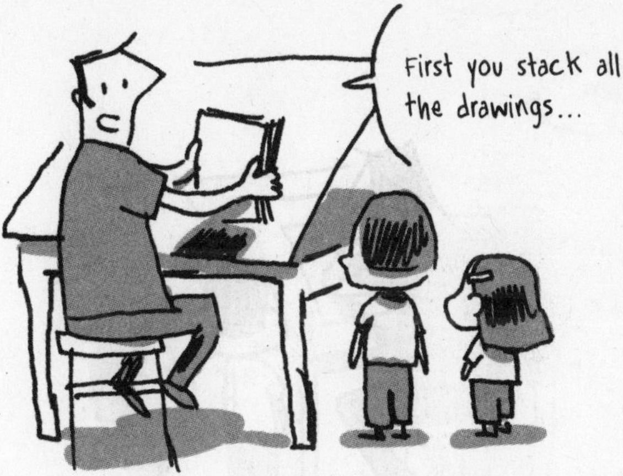
First you stack all the drawings...

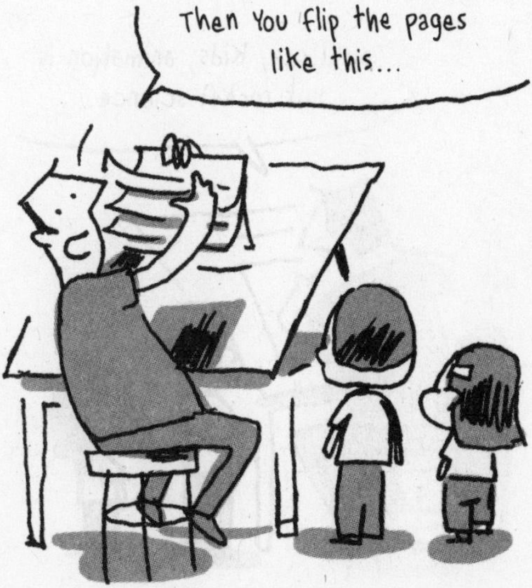
Then you flip the pages like this...

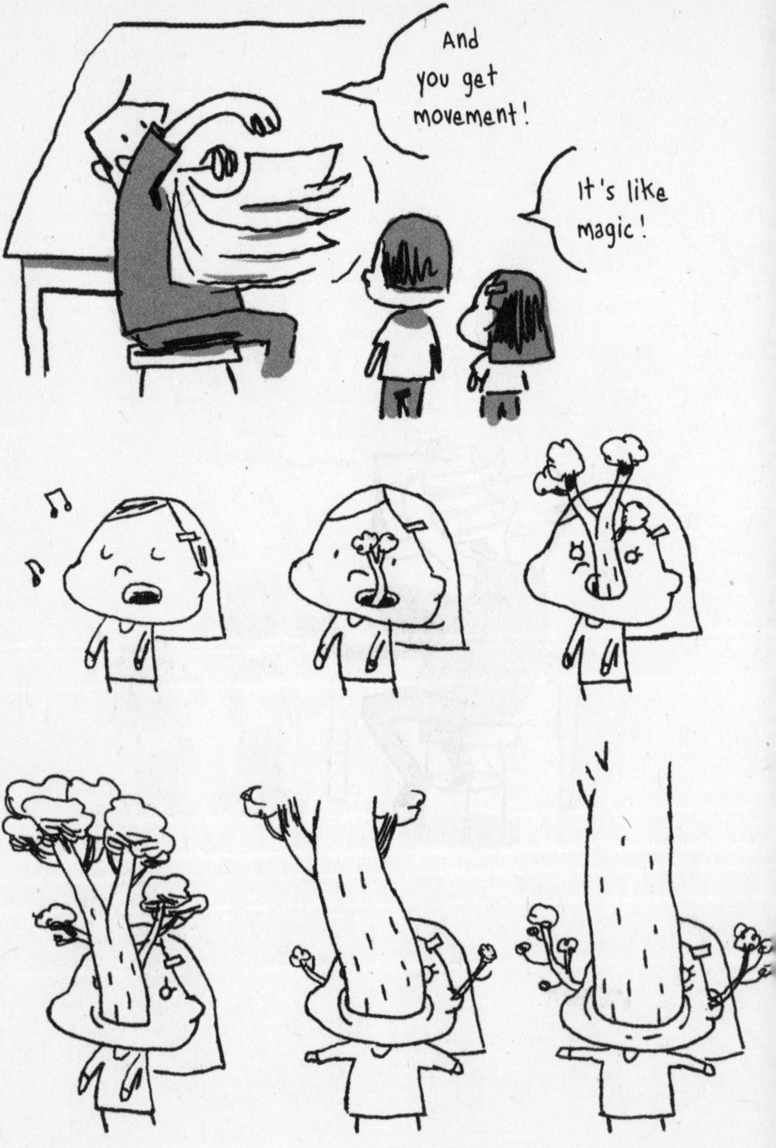
And you get movement!
It's like magic!

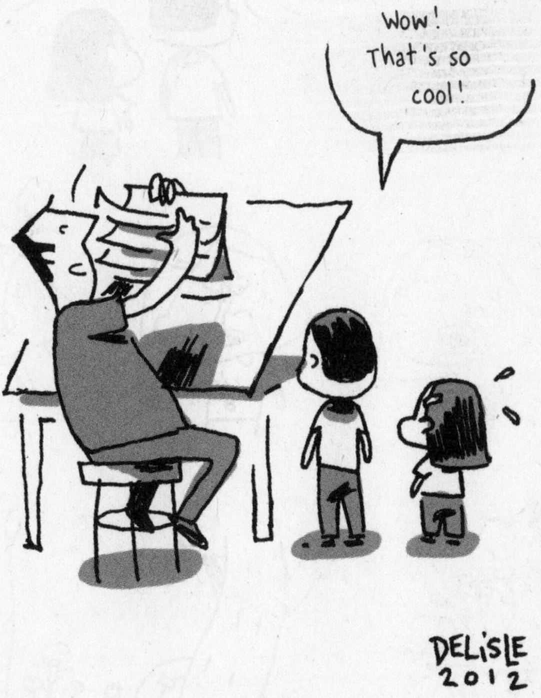
Wow! That's so cool!
DELISLE 2012

-Boxing

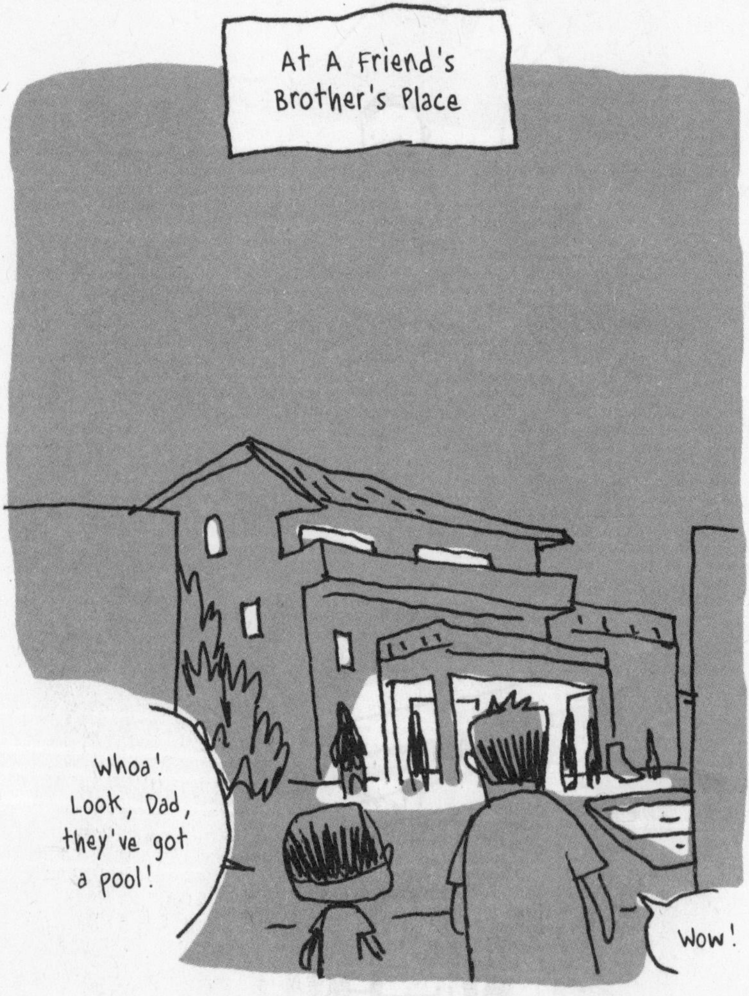
At A Friend's Brother's Place
Whoa! Look, Dad, they've got a pool!
Wow!

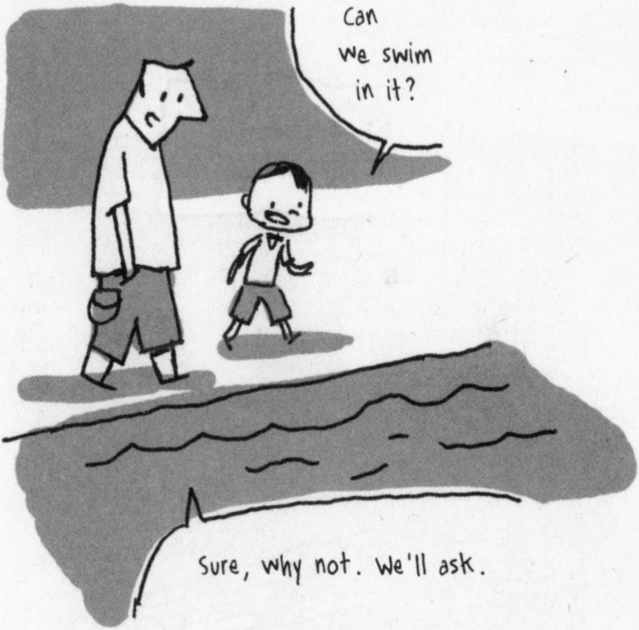
Can we swim in it?
Sure, why not. We'll ask.

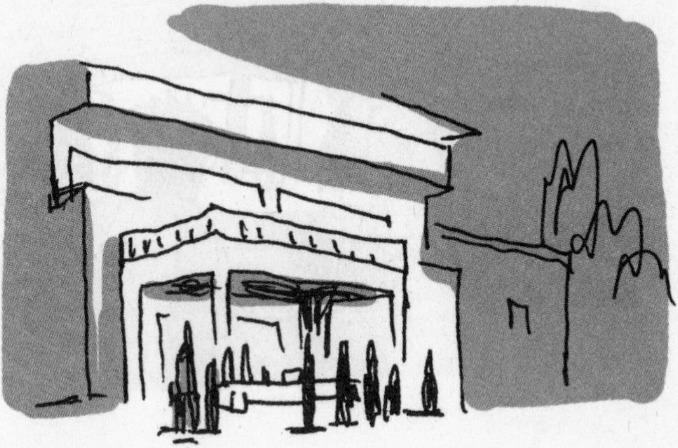

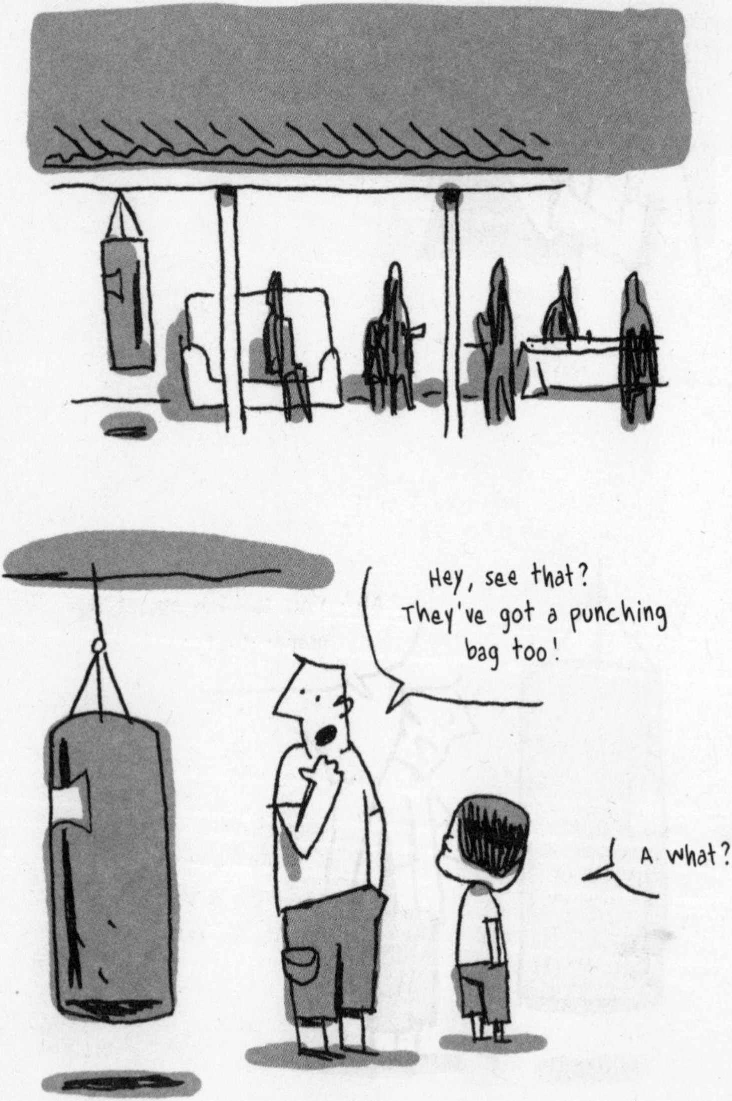
Hey, see that? They've got a punching bag too!
A what?

A punching bag!
To train for boxing.
You hit it with
your fists.

Ah! This reminds me of my
grandfather.

He had
one hanging
from a beam
in his barn.

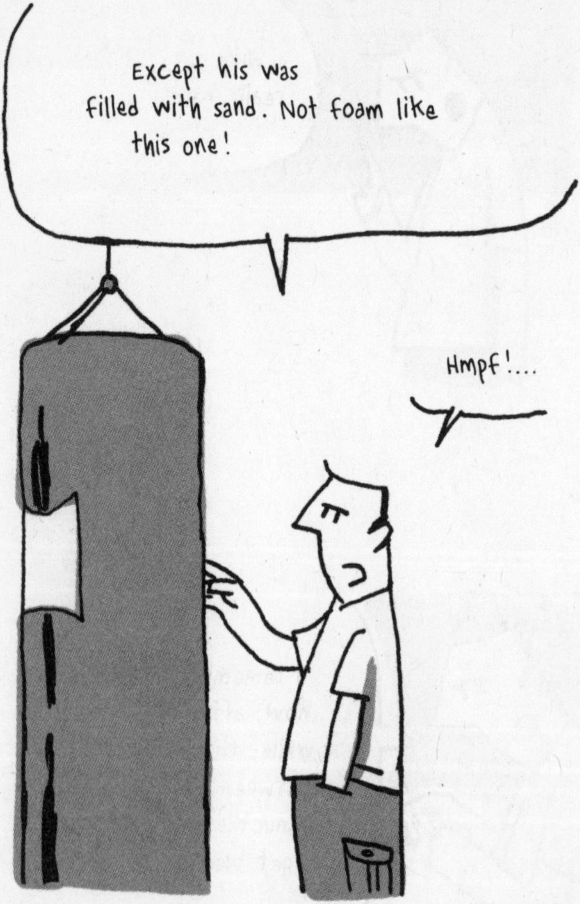
Except his was filled with sand. Not foam like this one!
Hmpf!...

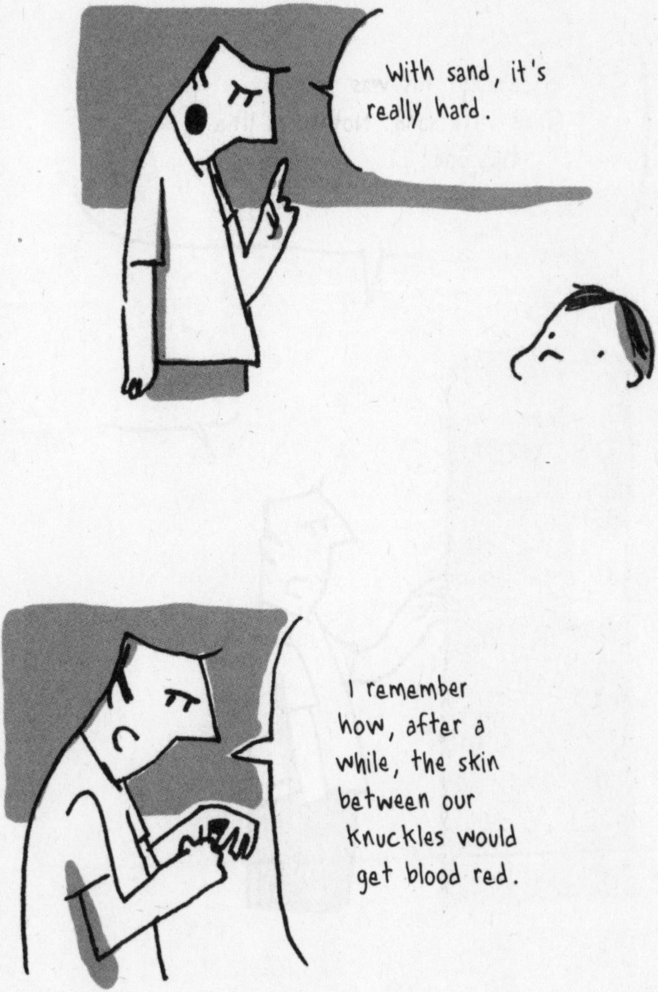
With sand, it's really hard.
I remember how, after a while, the skin between our knuckles would get blood red.

Blood red?

Yes, my boy...

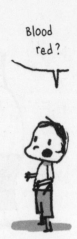

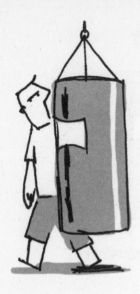

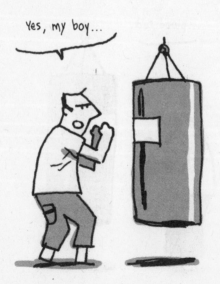

BAM!
...Blood red.

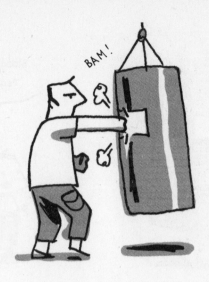

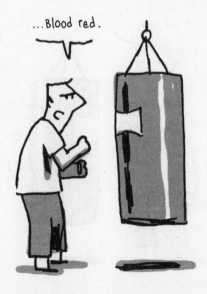

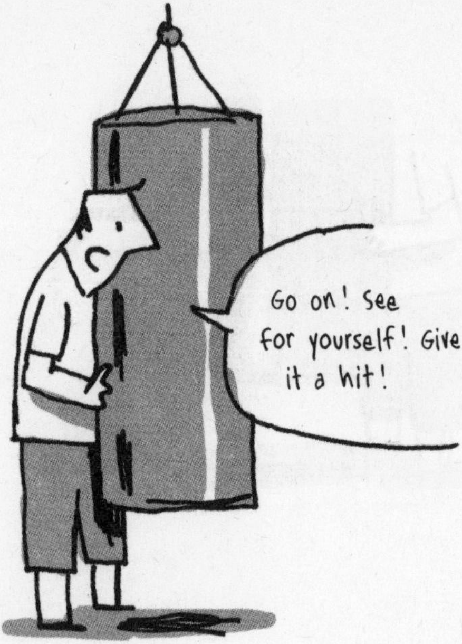
Go on! See for yourself! Give it a hit!

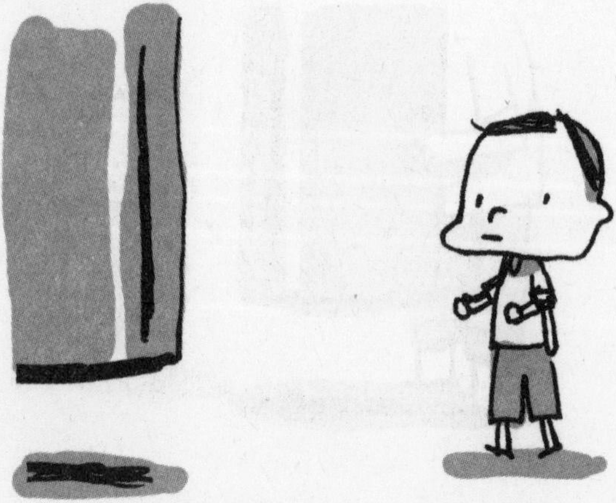

No, not like that!
Come on! Give it all you
got! Really hit it!

TAP

What kind of a punch was that?

You gotta stand like this!

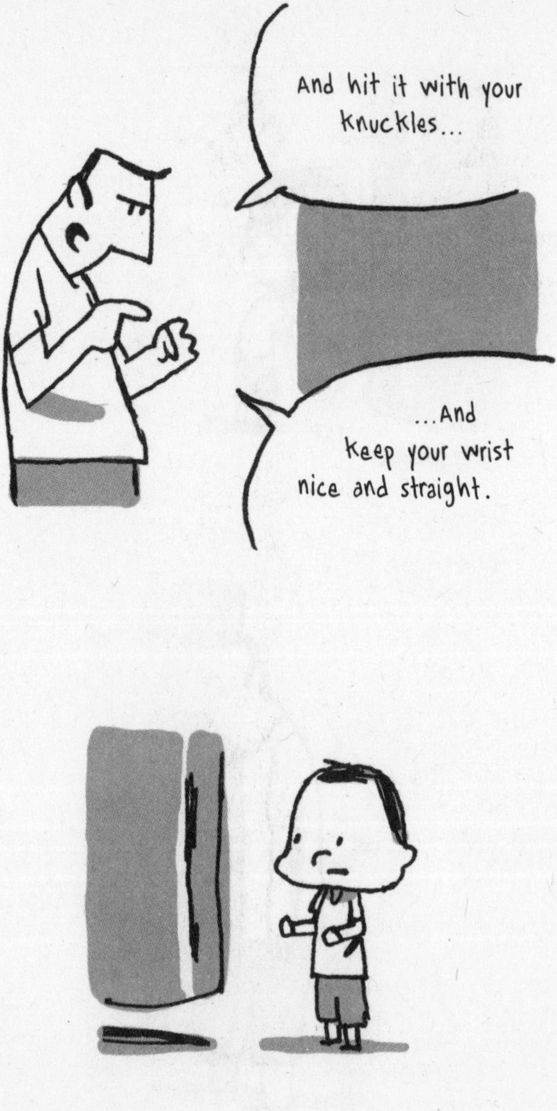
And hit it with your knuckles...
...And keep your wrist nice and straight.

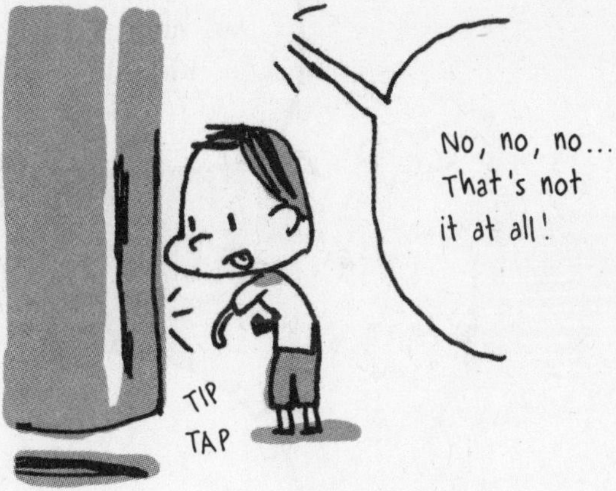
No, no, no...
That's not
it at all!
TIP
TAP

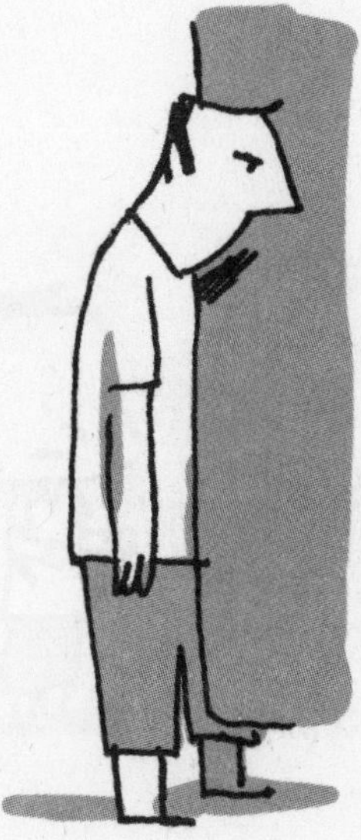

Okay...
We're going
to try some-
thing else.

Imagine you're hitting
someone...

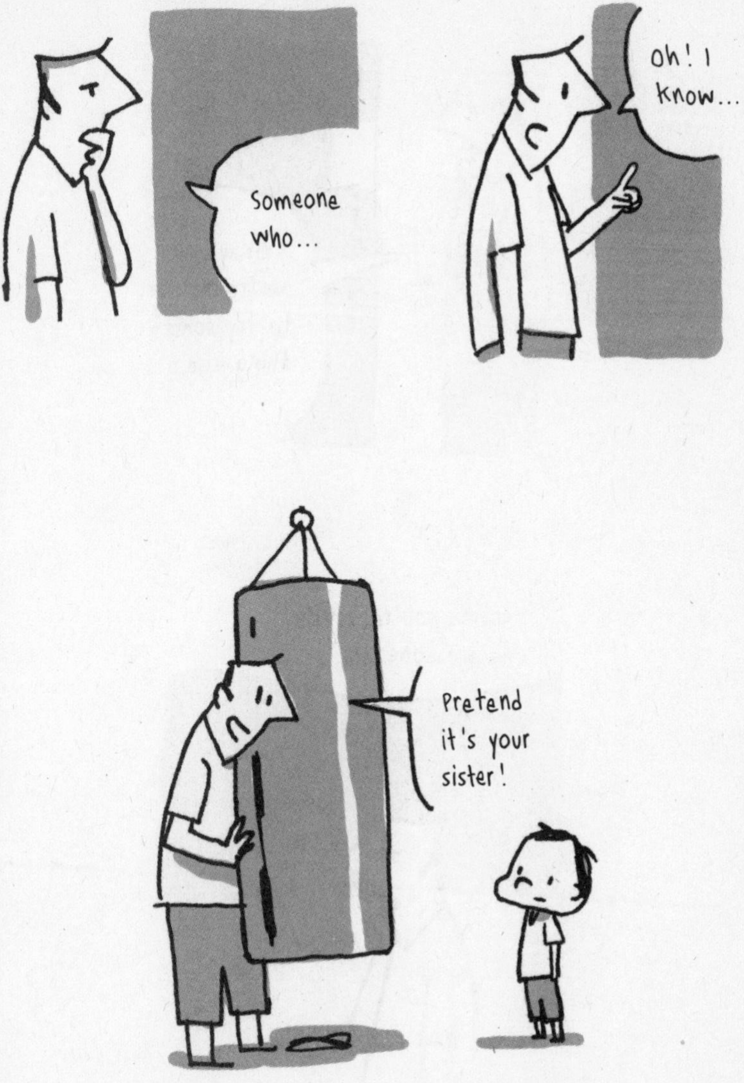
Someone who...
Oh! I know...
Pretend it's your sister!

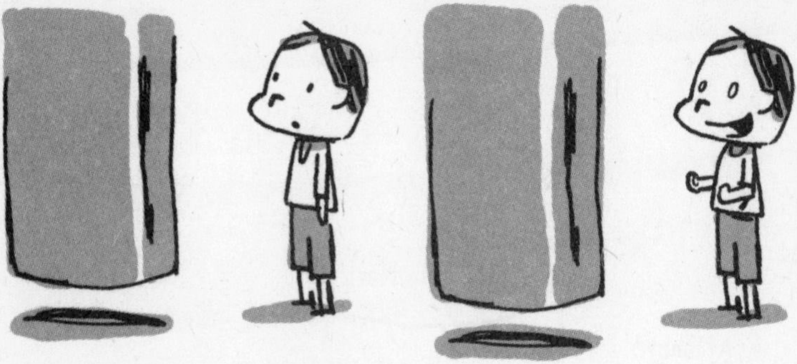

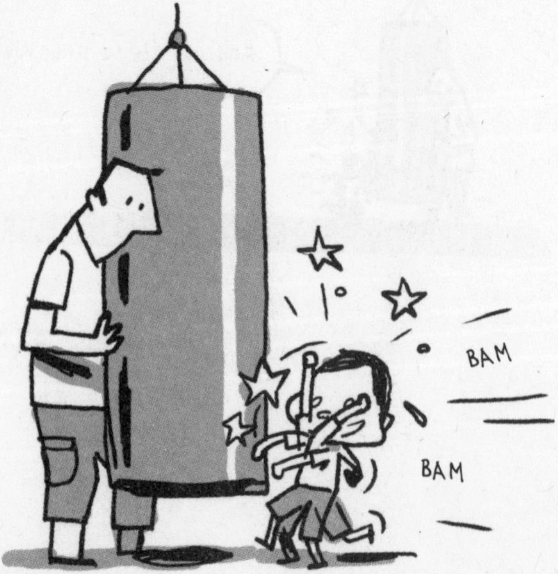
BAM
BAM

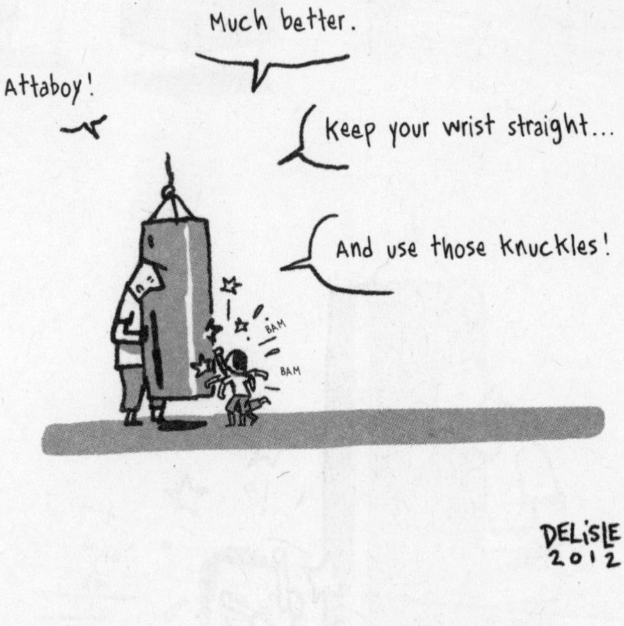
Attaboy!
Much better.
Keep your wrist straight...
And use those knuckles!
BAM
BAM
DELISLE 2012

-The Gifts

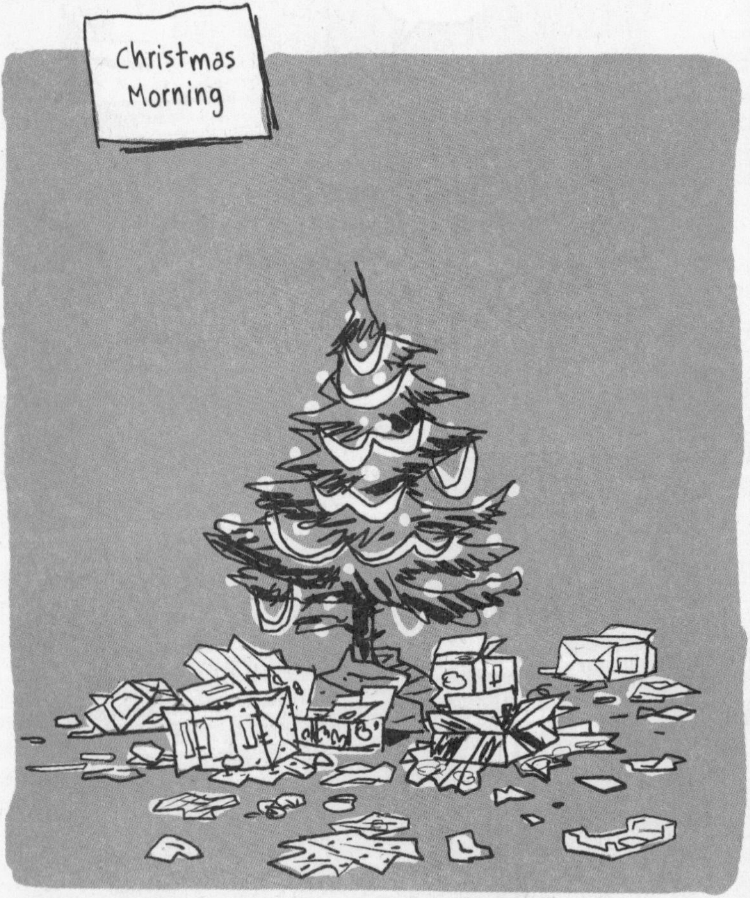
Christmas Morning

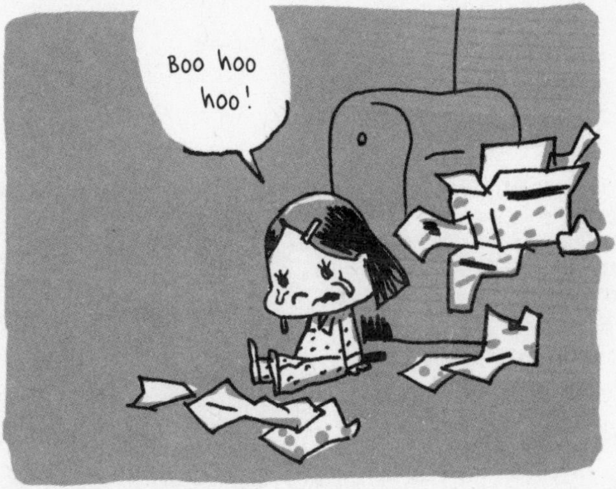
Boo hoo hoo!

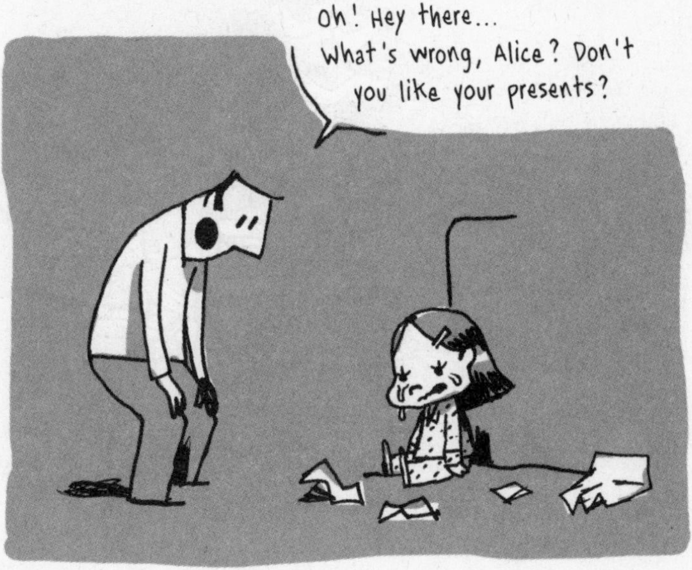
Oh! Hey there... What's wrong, Alice? Don't you like your presents?

How come you're crying? It's Christmas—you should be happy!

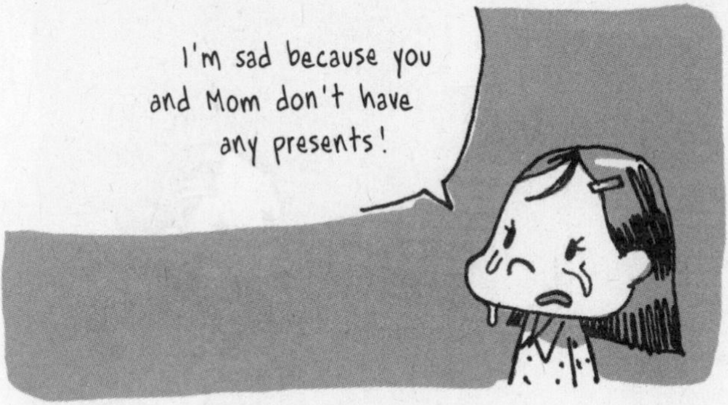
I'm sad because you and Mom don't have any presents!

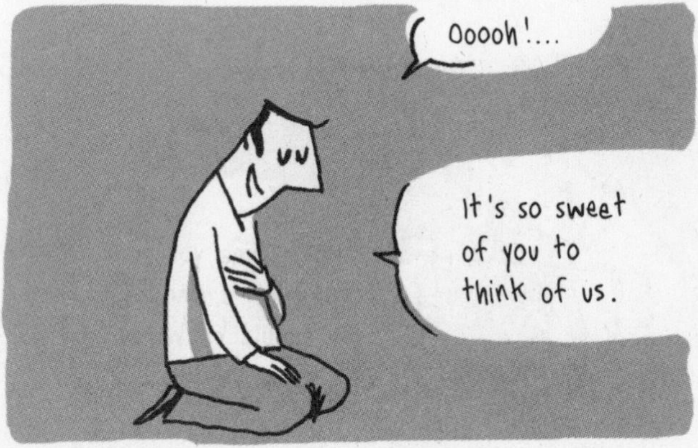
Ooooh!...
It's so sweet of you to think of us.

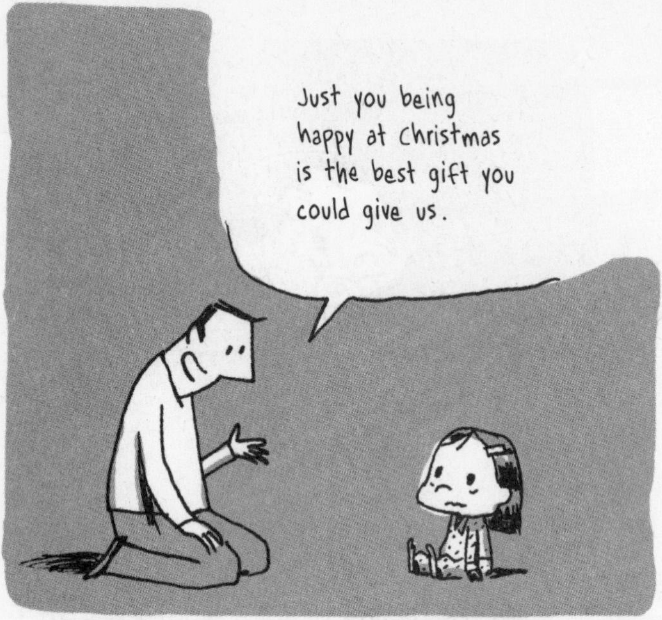
Just you being happy at Christmas is the best gift you could give us.

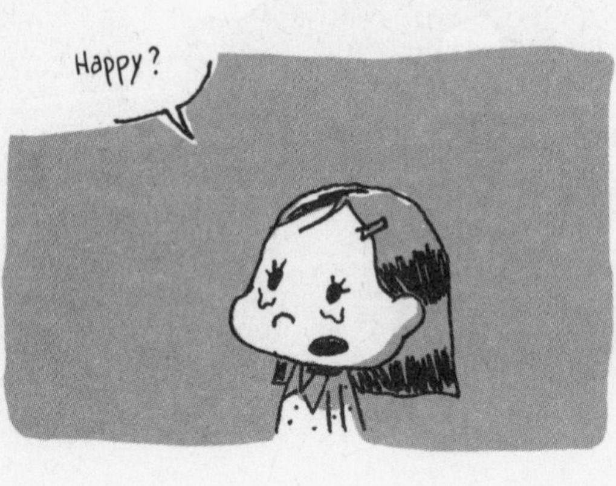
Happy?

BOO
hoo
hoo!

DELISLE
2012

-The Little Mouse

So, did that little mouse come by
last night and leave some money
under your pillow?

Yes,
but...

I still think there's something weird about the whole mouse story...

Where does it come from?

Is there a hole somewhere in the house?

And how does the mouse know
there's a tooth under
my pillow?

Does it have a super-developed
sense of smell?

Last time, what did it
leave—fifty cents?

And you thought that
wasn't a lot...

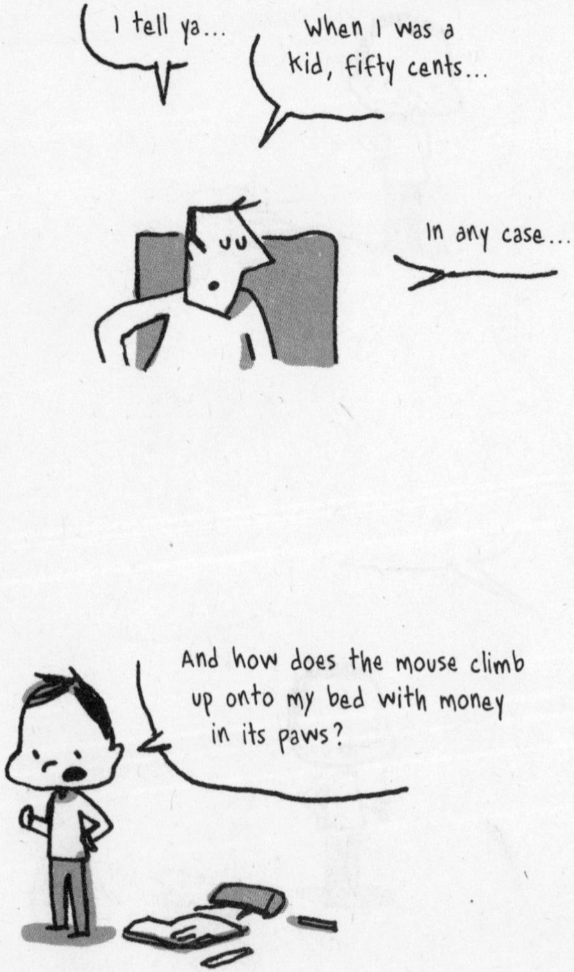
I tell ya...
When I was a kid, fifty cents...
In any case...
And how does the mouse climb up onto my bed with money in its paws?

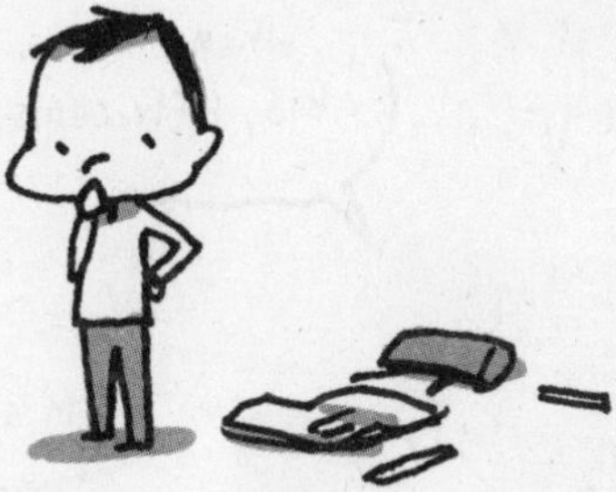

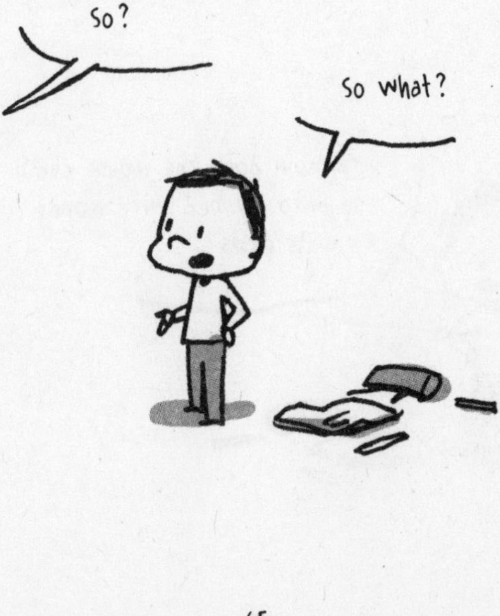
So?
So what?

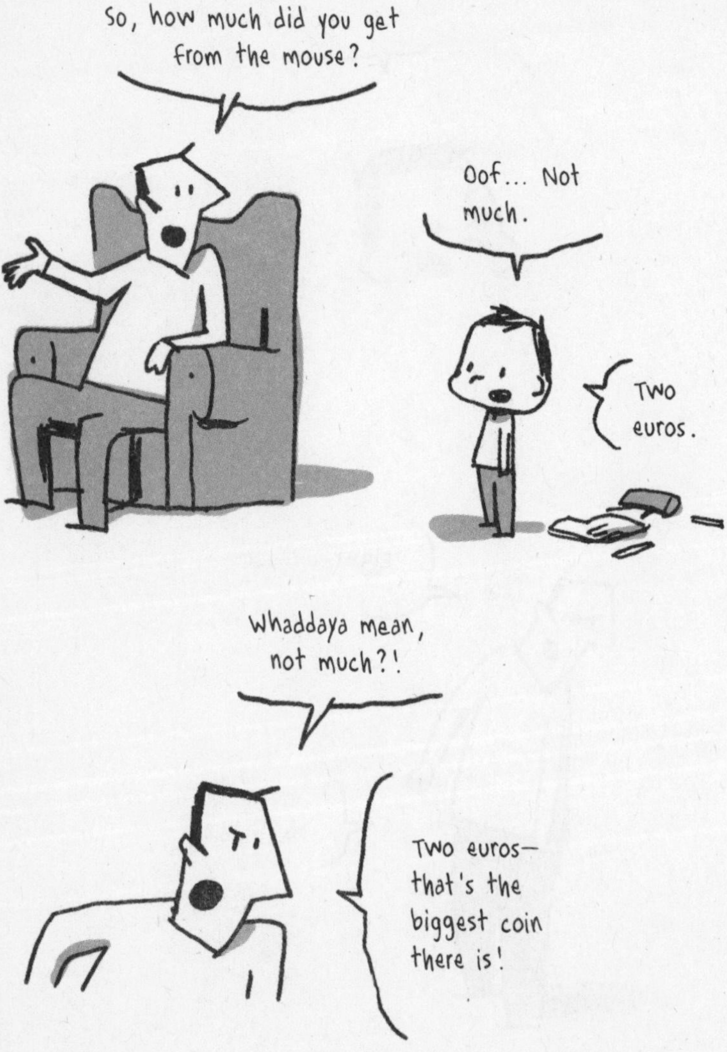
So, how much did you get from the mouse?
Oof... Not much.
Two euros.
Whaddaya mean, not much?!
Two euros— that's the biggest coin there is!

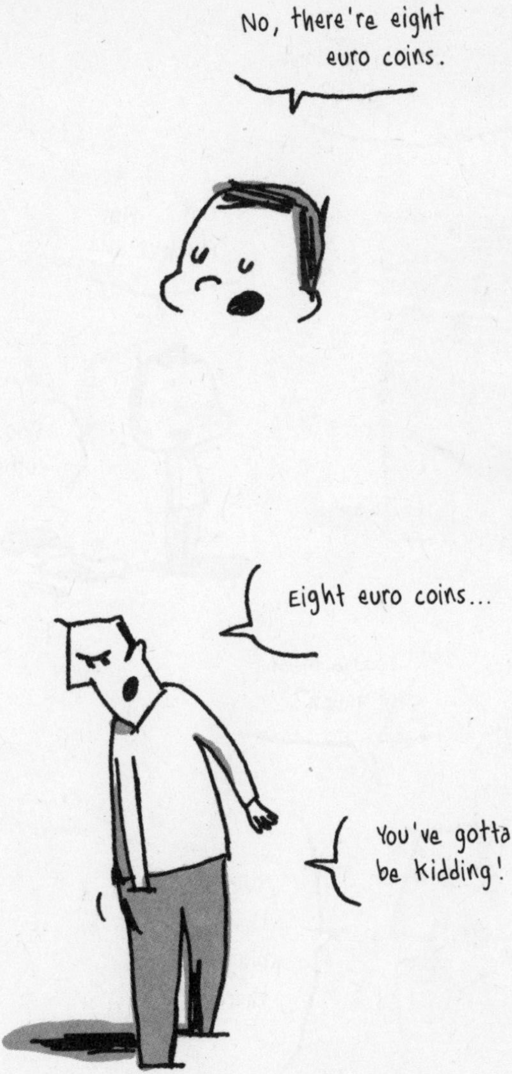
No, there're eight euro coins.
Eight euro coins...
You've gotta be kidding!

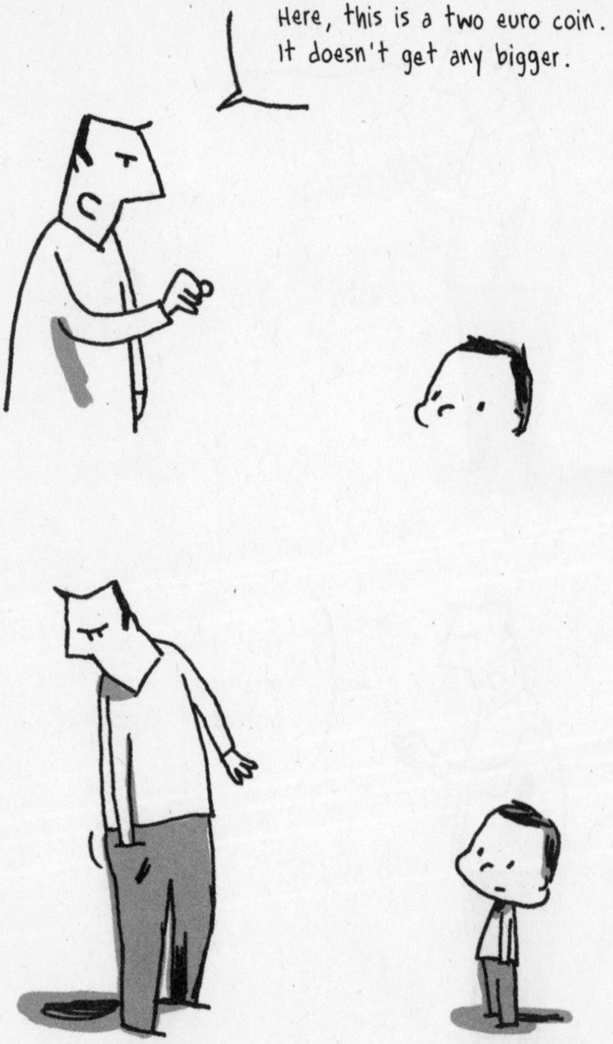
Here, this is a two euro coin.
It doesn't get any bigger.

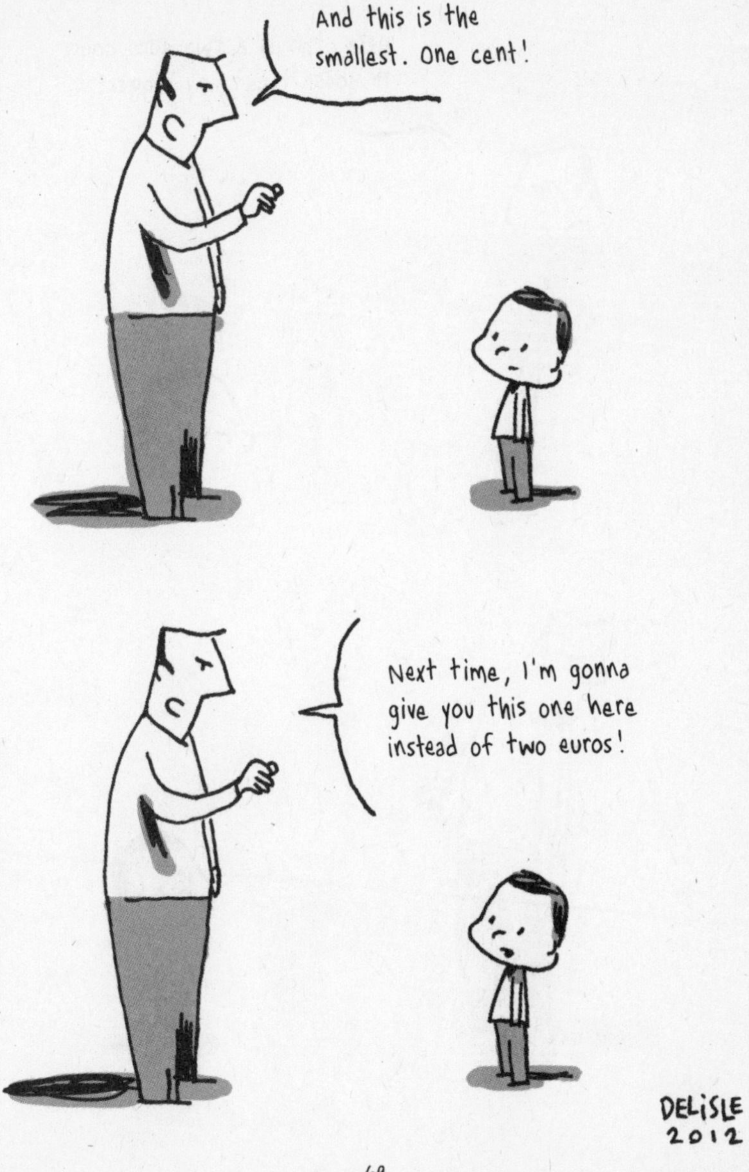
And this is the smallest. One cent!
Next time, I'm gonna give you this one here instead of two euros!
DELISLE 2012

-The Monkey

Morning
Good God!

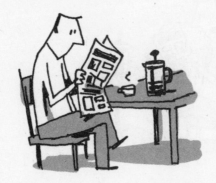

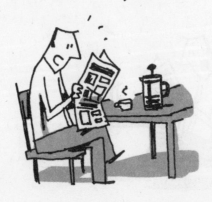

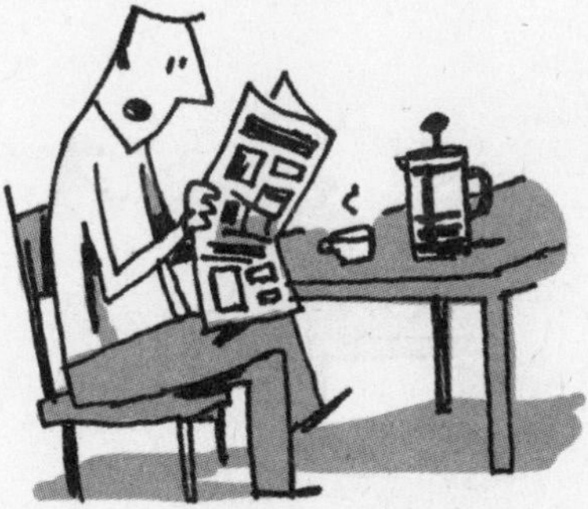

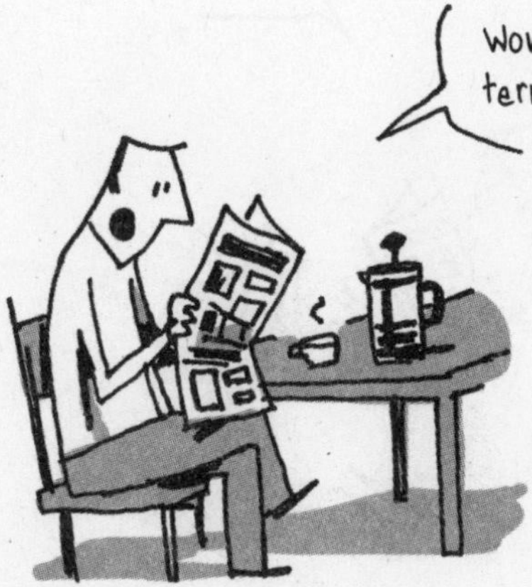
Wow, that's terrible!

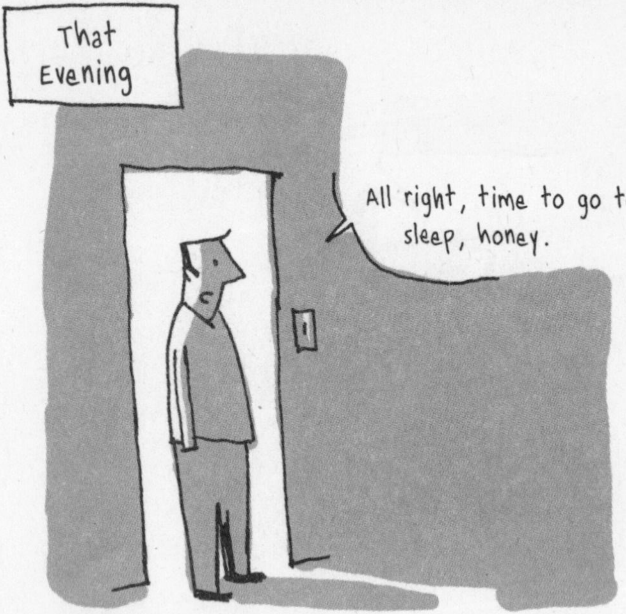
That Evening
All right, time to go to sleep, honey.

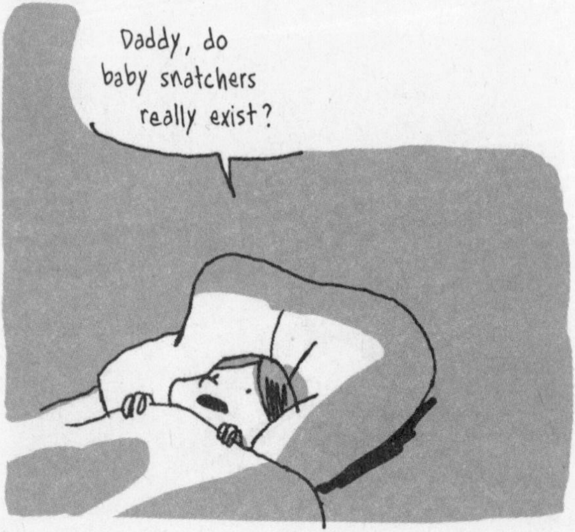
Daddy, do baby snatchers really exist?

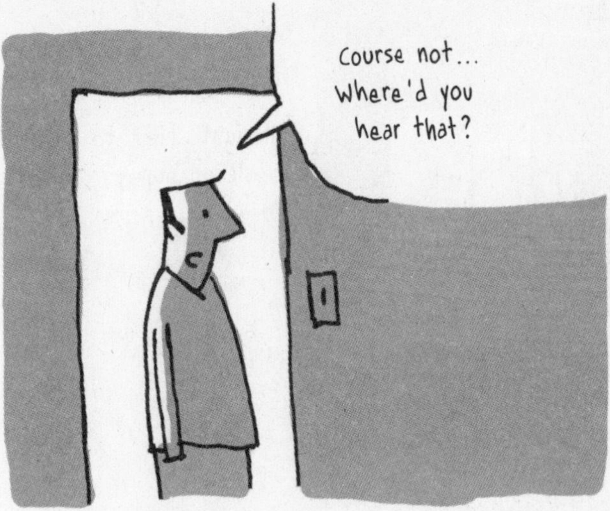
Course not...
Where'd you
hear that?

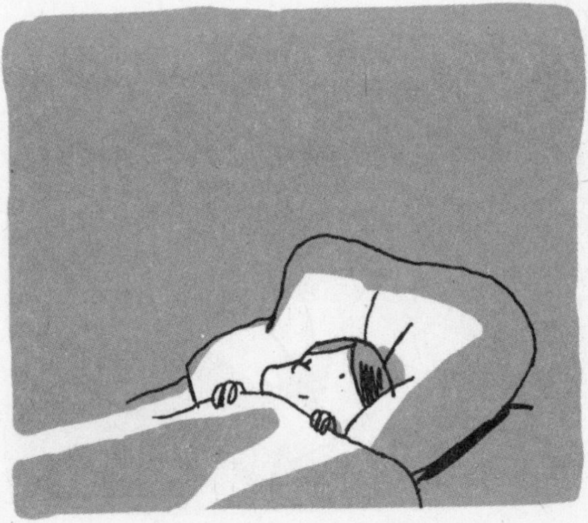

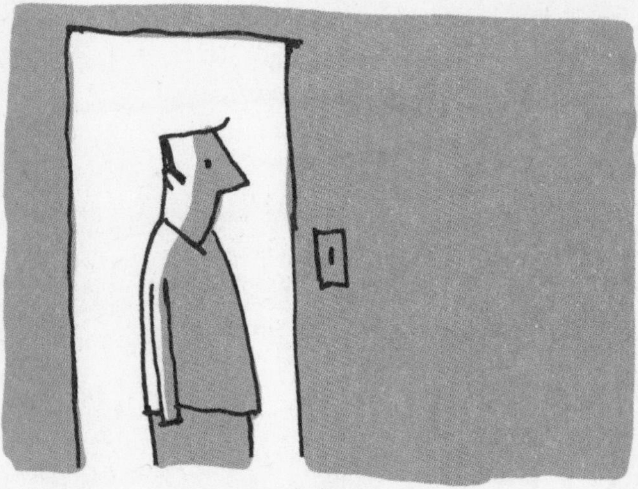

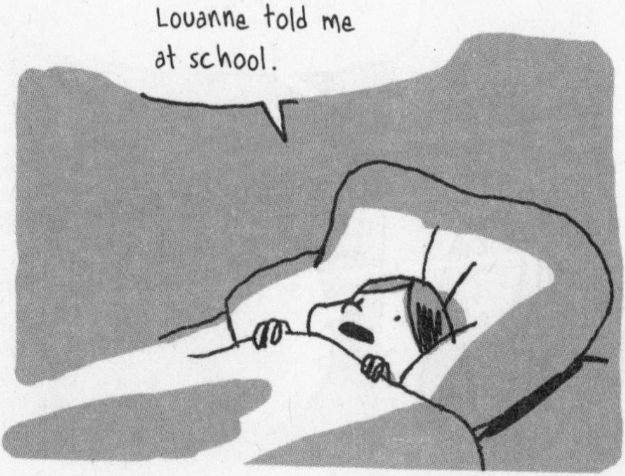
Louanne told me at school.

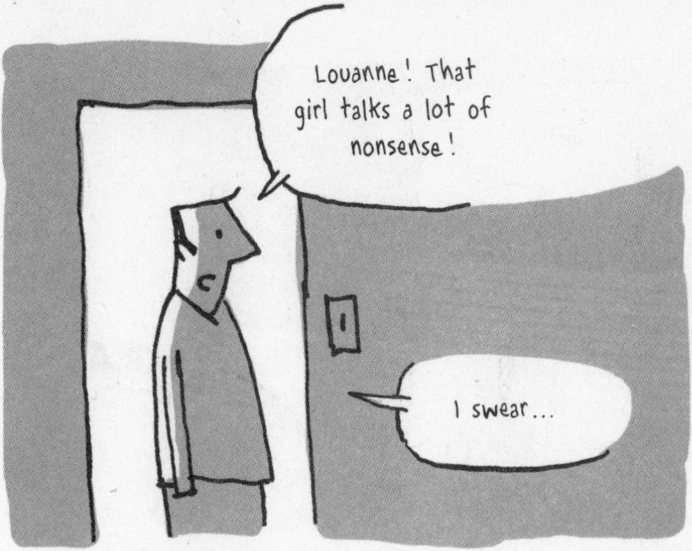
Louanne! That girl talks a lot of nonsense!
I swear...

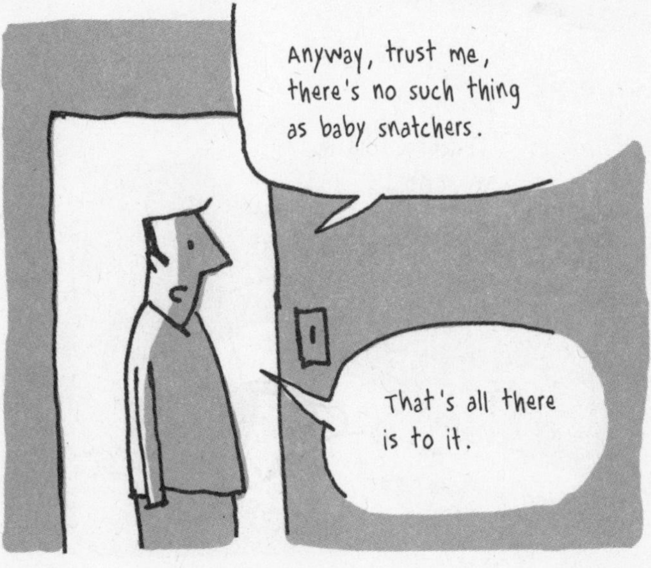
Anyway, trust me, there's no such thing as baby snatchers.
That's all there is to it.

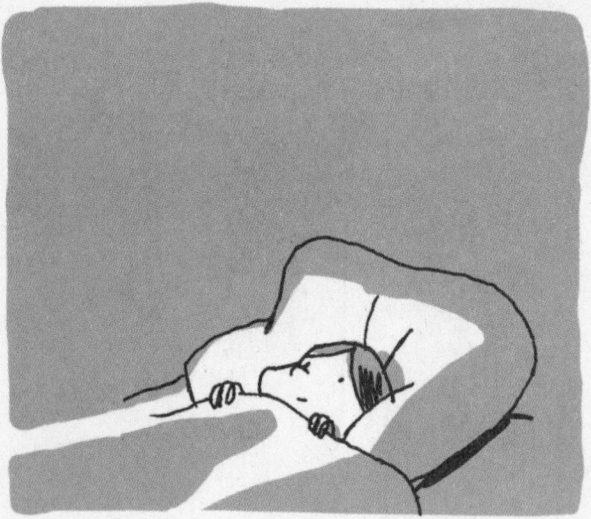

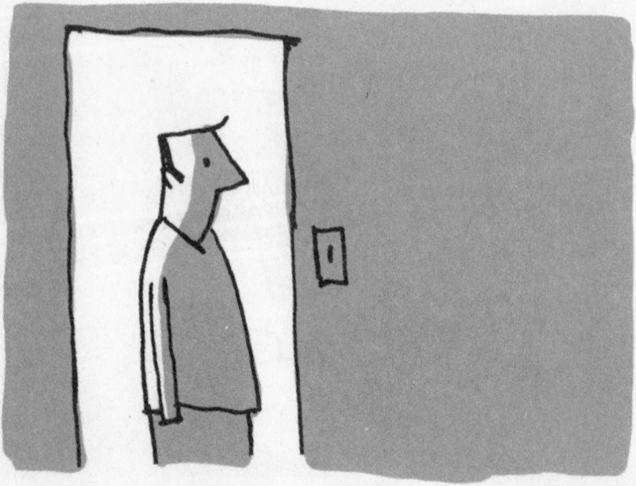

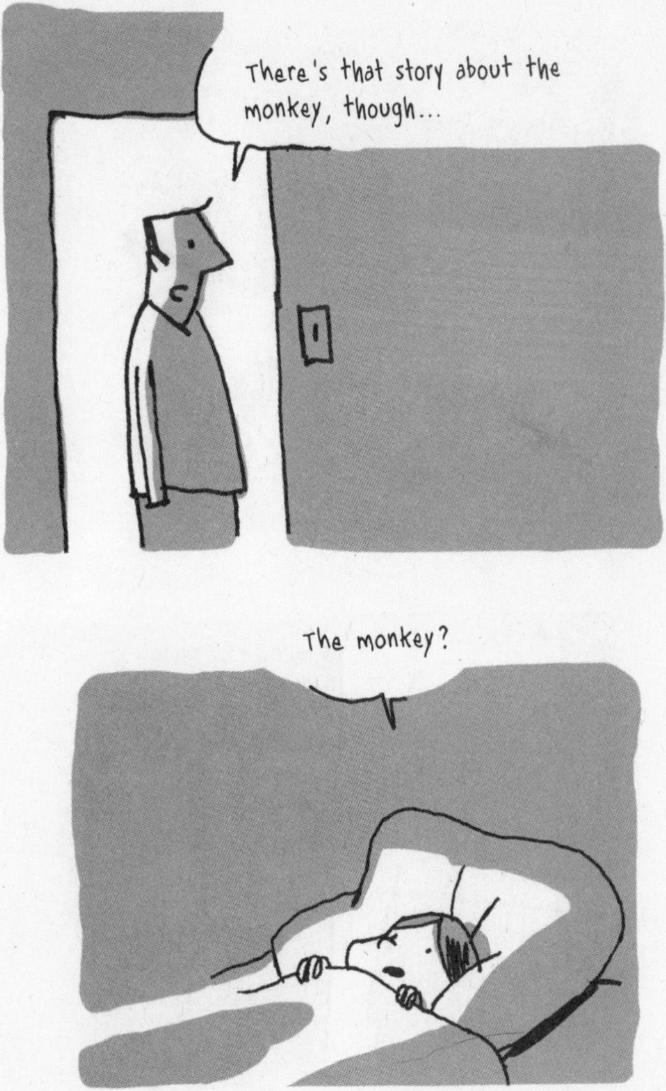
There's that story about the monkey, though...
The monkey?

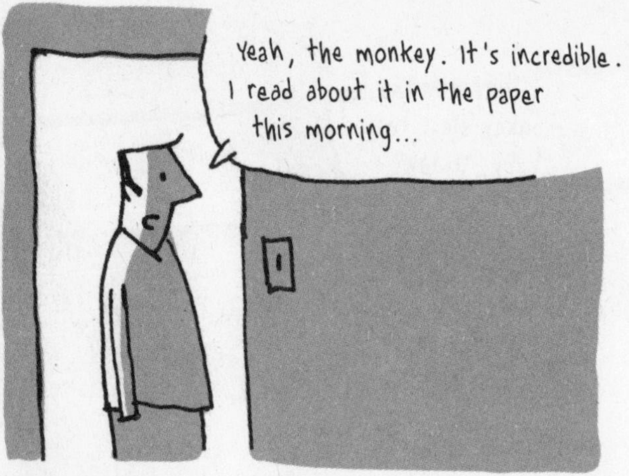

Yeah, the monkey. It's incredible. I read about it in the paper this morning...

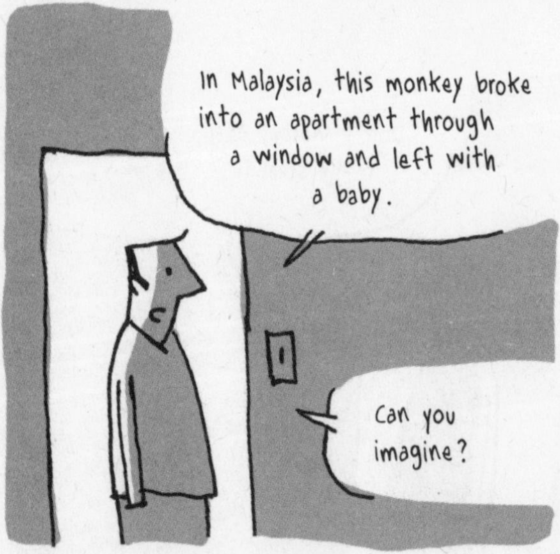

In Malaysia, this monkey broke into an apartment through a window and left with a baby.
Can you imagine?

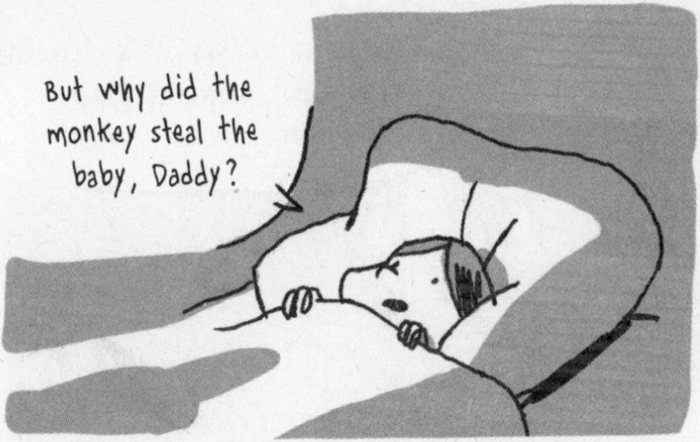
But why did the monkey steal the baby, Daddy?

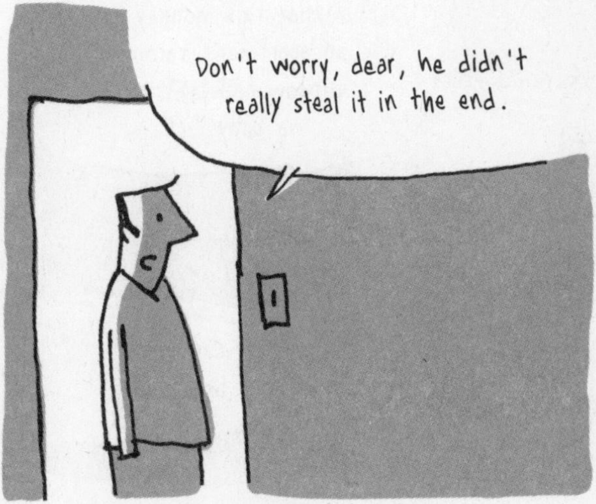
Don't worry, dear, he didn't really steal it in the end.

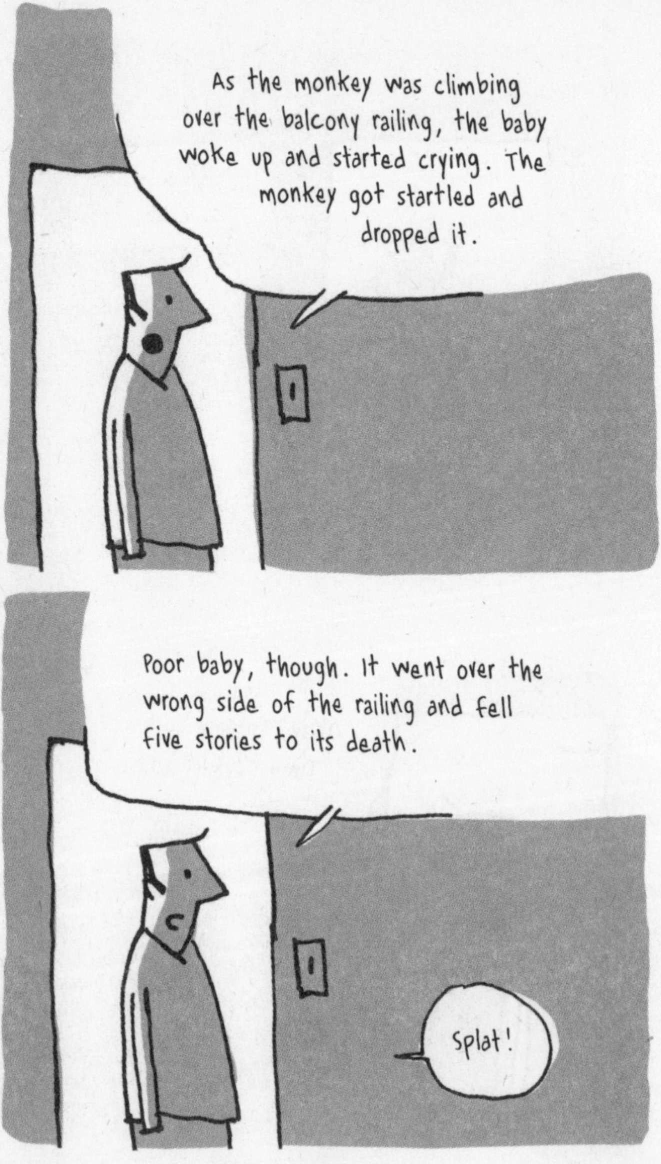
As the monkey was climbing over the balcony railing, the baby woke up and started crying. The monkey got startled and dropped it.
Poor baby, though. It went over the wrong side of the railing and fell five stories to its death.
Splat!

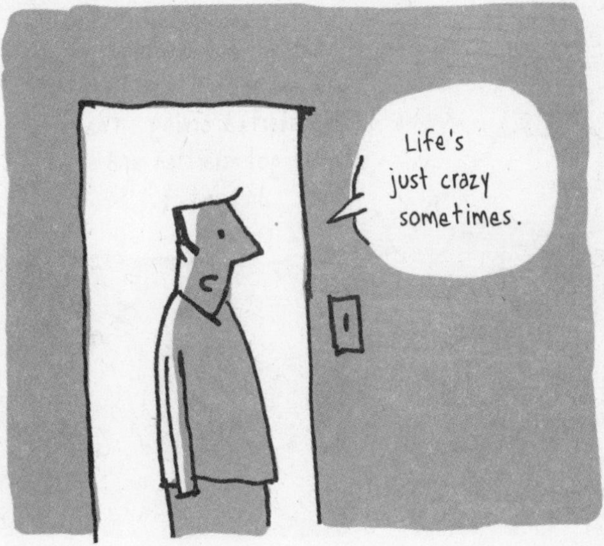
Life's just crazy sometimes.

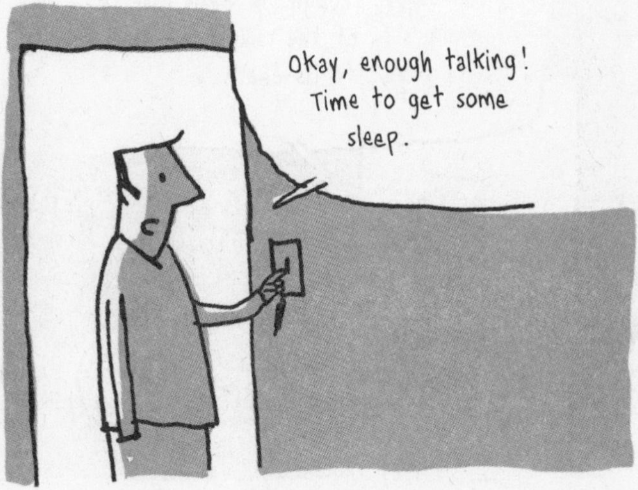
Okay, enough talking! Time to get some sleep.

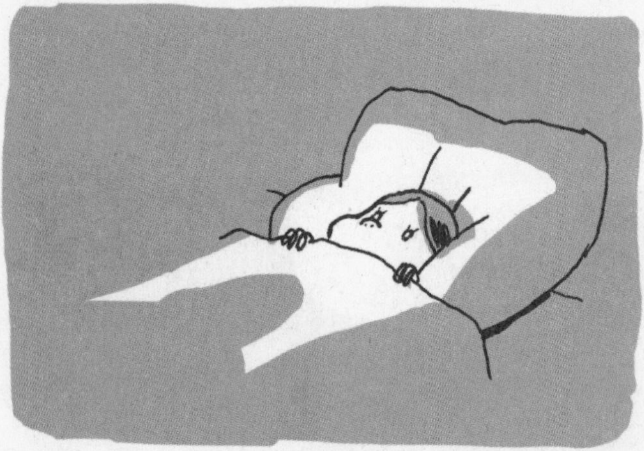

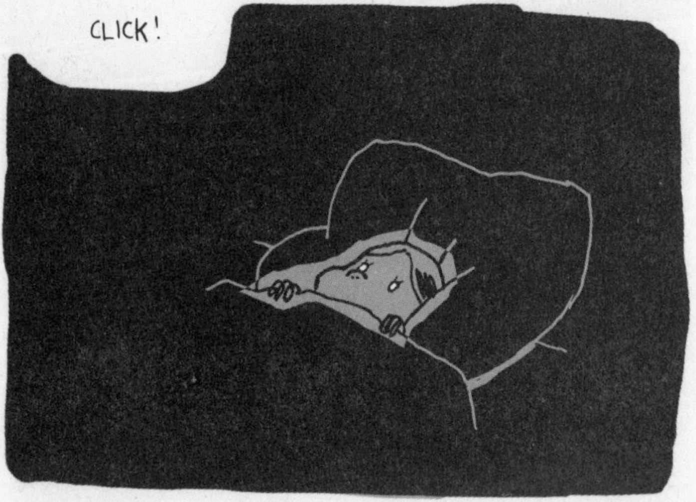
CLICK!

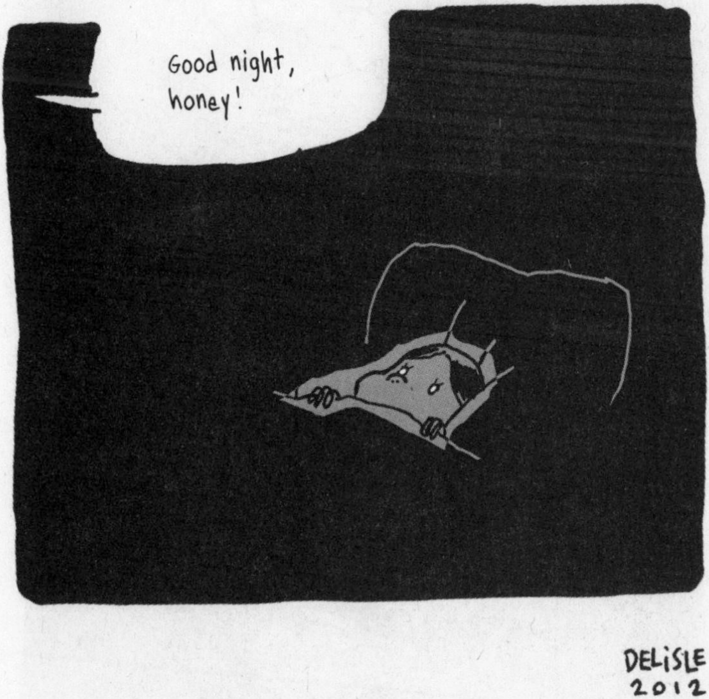
Good night, honey!
DELISLE 2012

-The Chainsaw

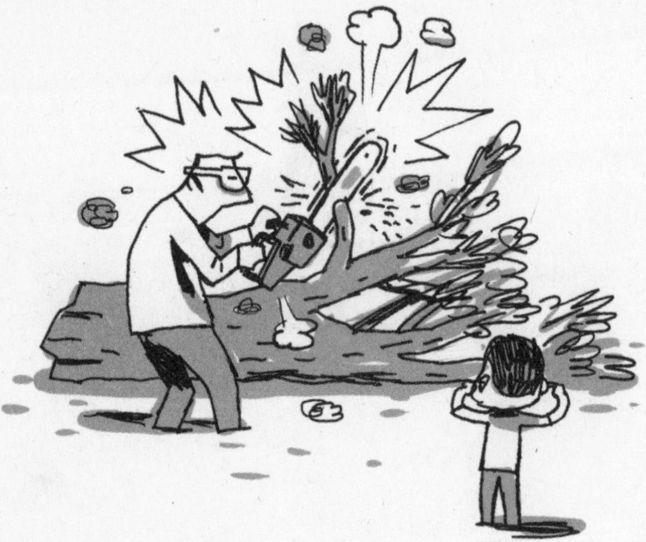

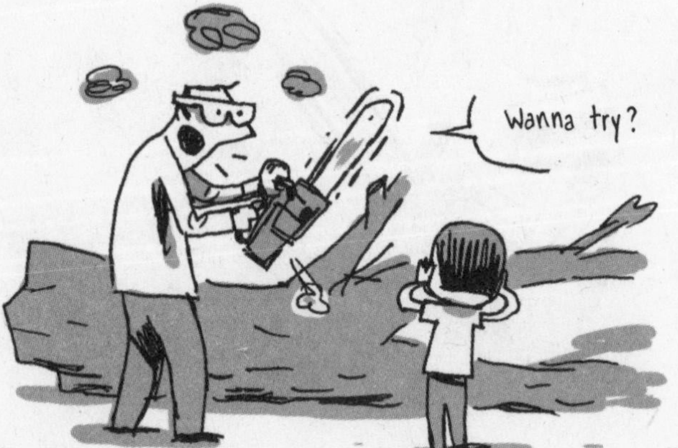
Wanna try?

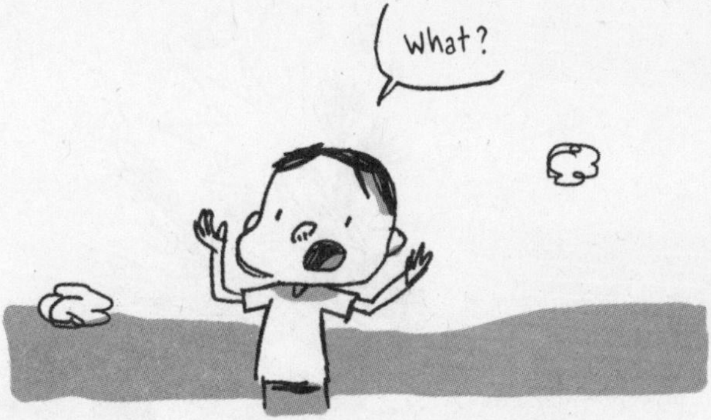
what?

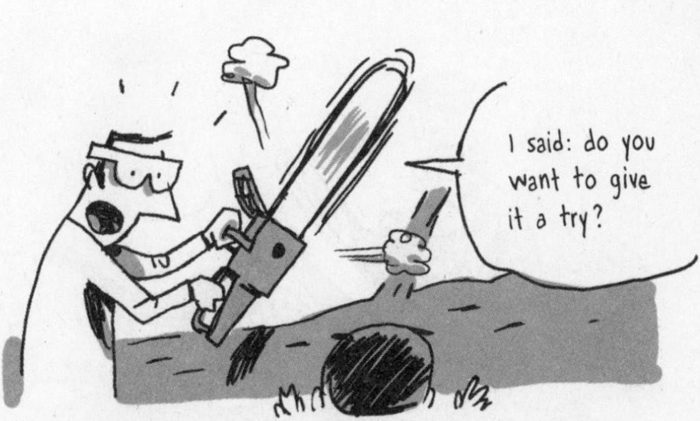
I said: do you want to give it a try?

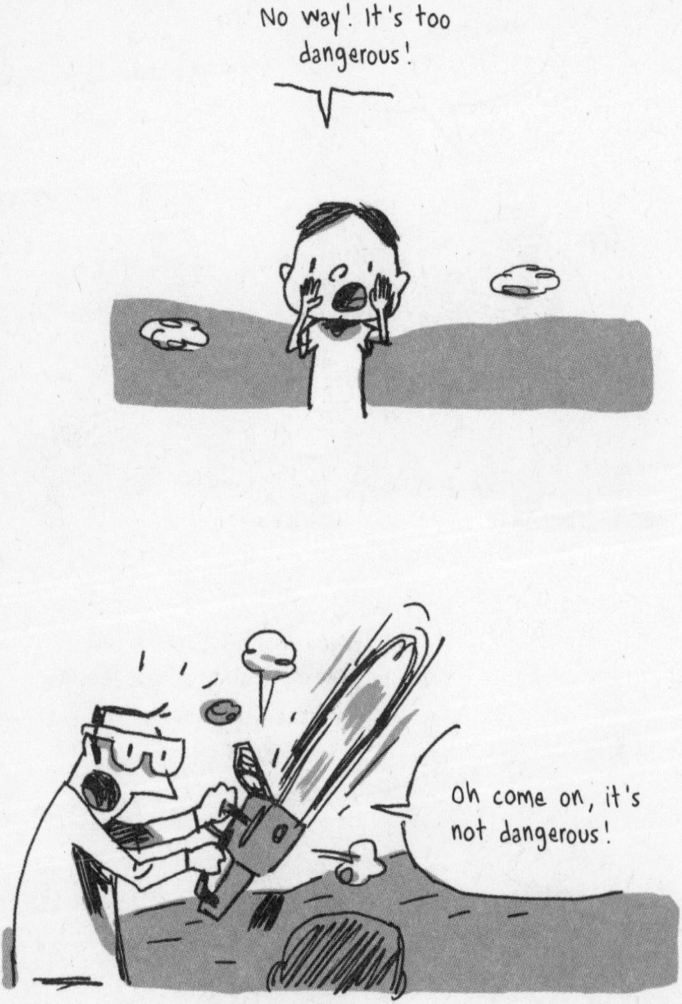
No way! It's too dangerous!
Oh come on, it's not dangerous!

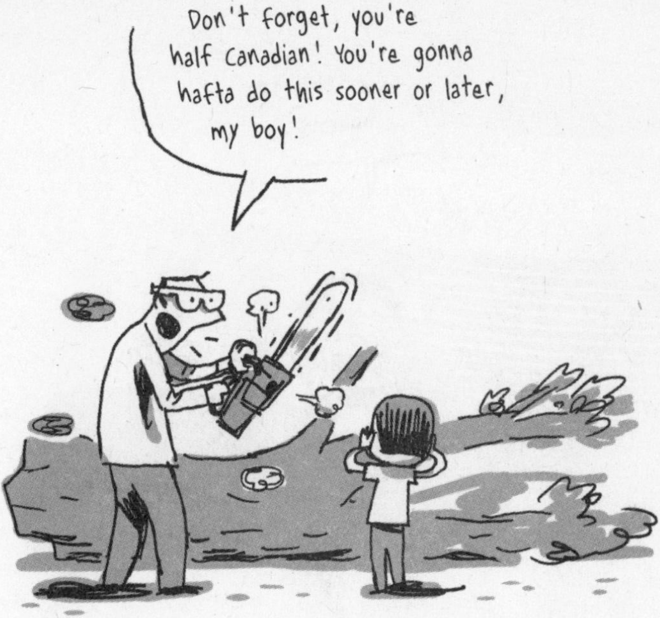
Don't forget, you're half Canadian! You're gonna hafta do this sooner or later, my boy!

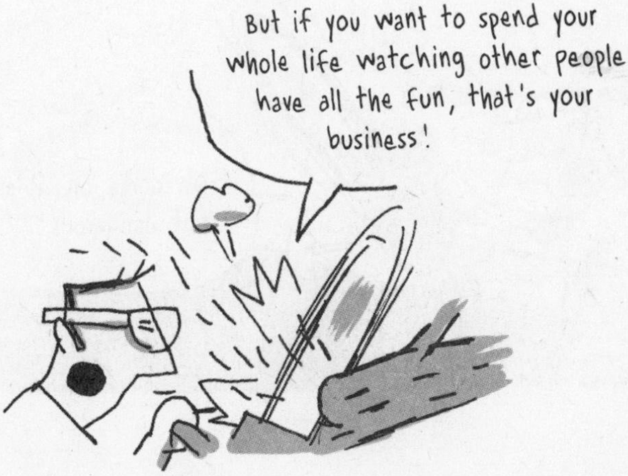
But if you want to spend your whole life watching other people have all the fun, that's your business!

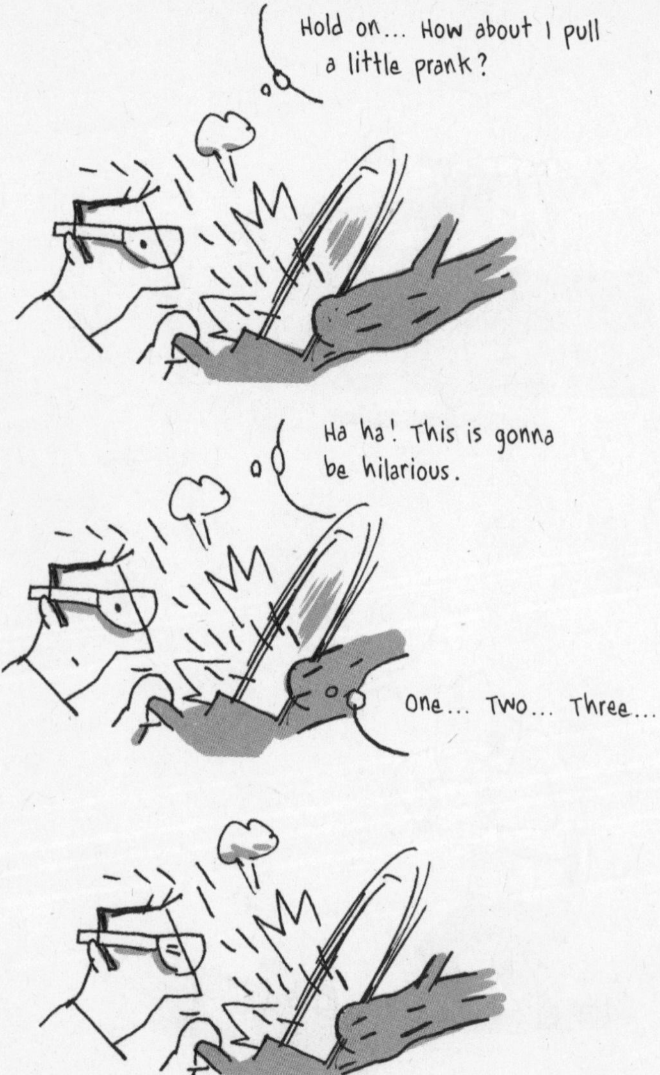
Hold on... How about I pull a little prank?
Ha ha! This is gonna be hilarious.
One... Two... Three...

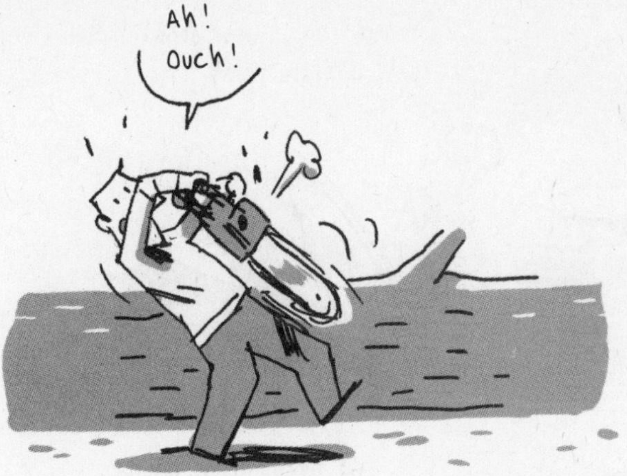
Ah!
Ouch!

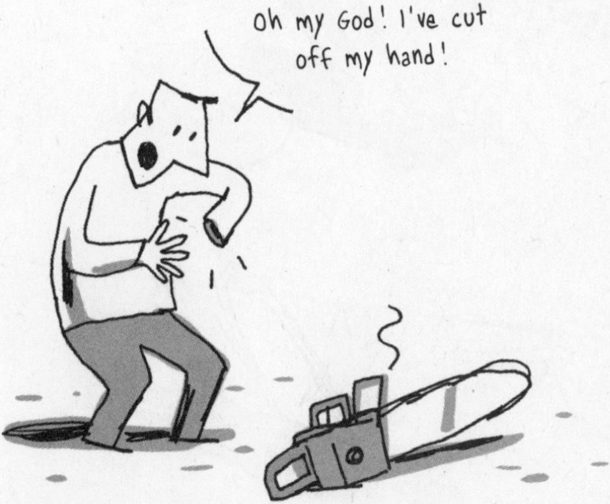
Oh my God! I've cut off my hand!

Mom!
Mom!

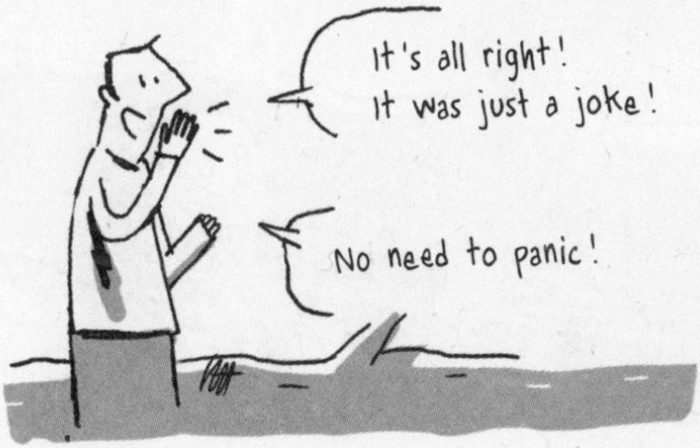
It's all right!
It was just a joke!
No need to panic!

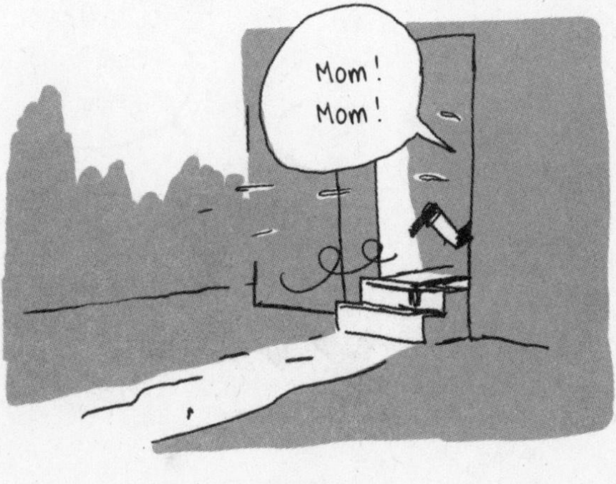
Mom!
Mom!

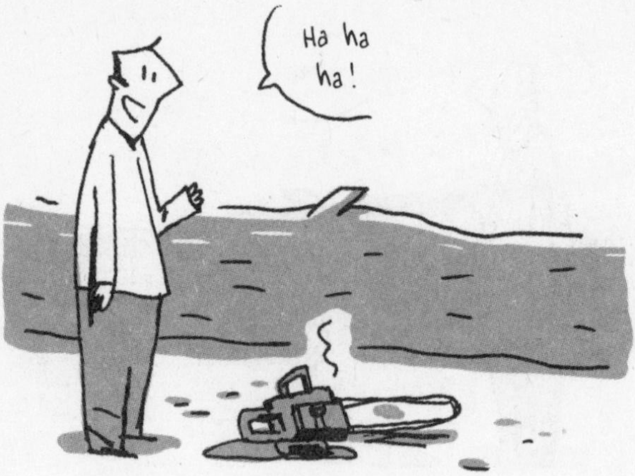
Ha ha ha!

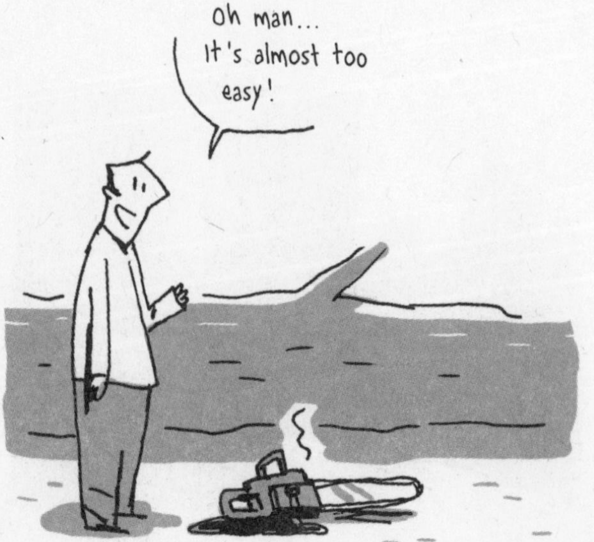
Oh man... It's almost too easy!

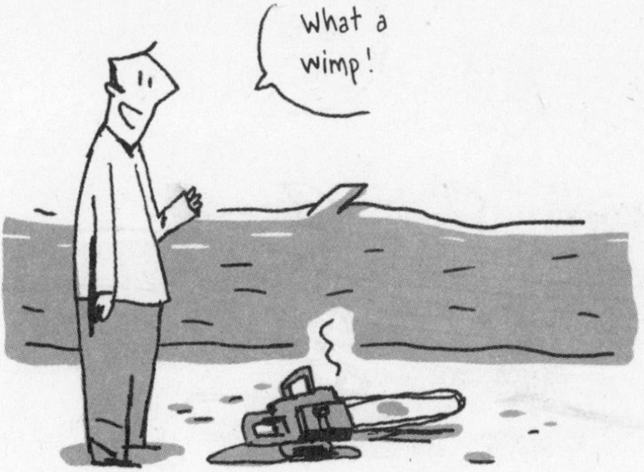
What a wimp!

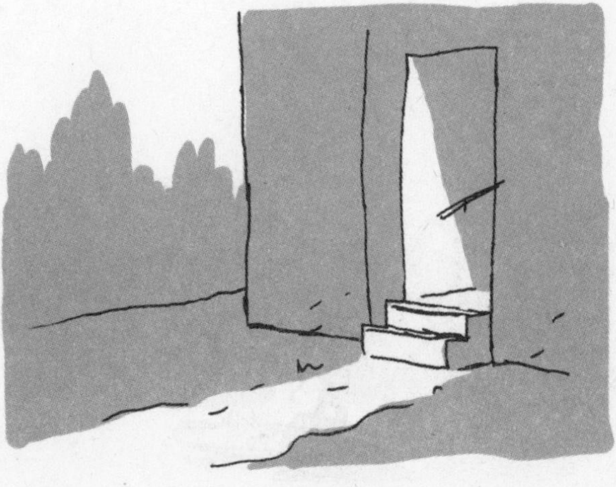

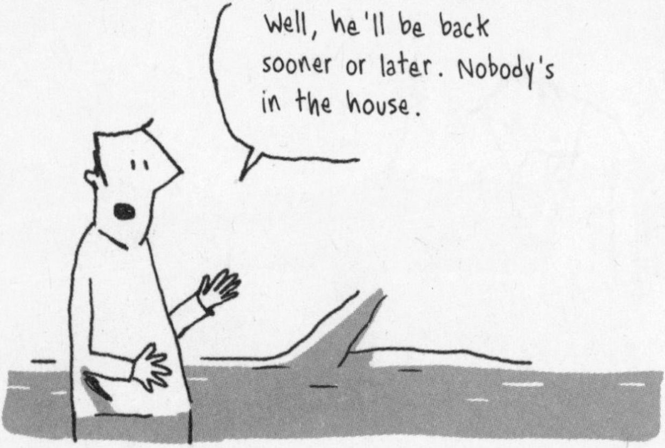
Well, he'll be back sooner or later. Nobody's in the house.

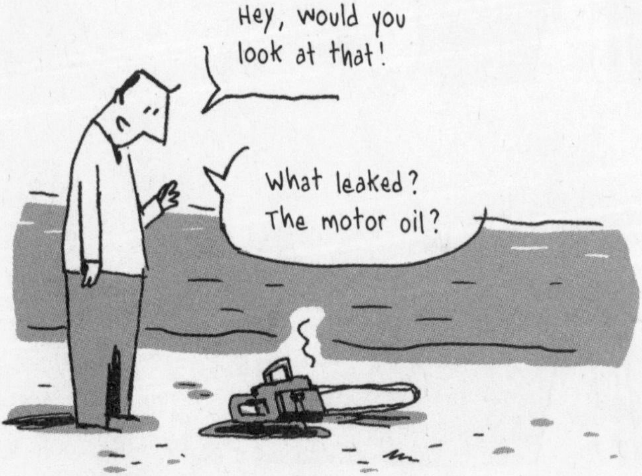
Hey, would you look at that!
What leaked? The motor oil?

I never knew chainsaw oil was so red.

It almost looks like blood...

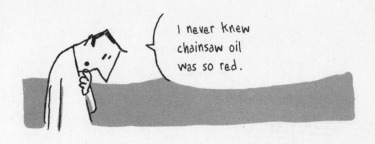

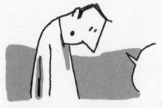

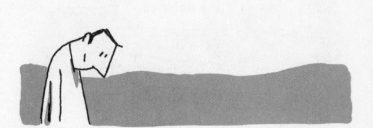

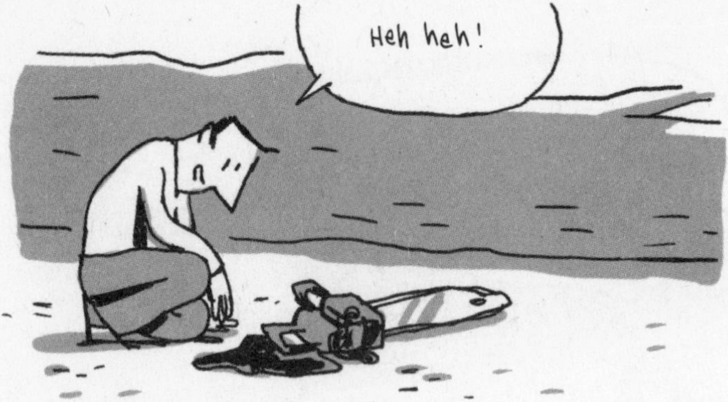
Heh heh!

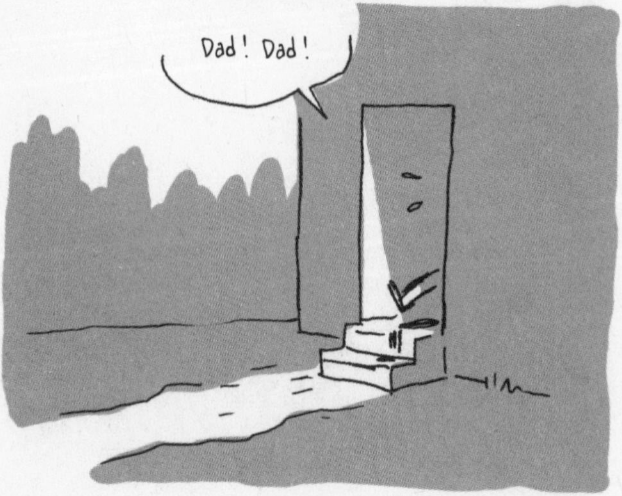
Dad! Dad!

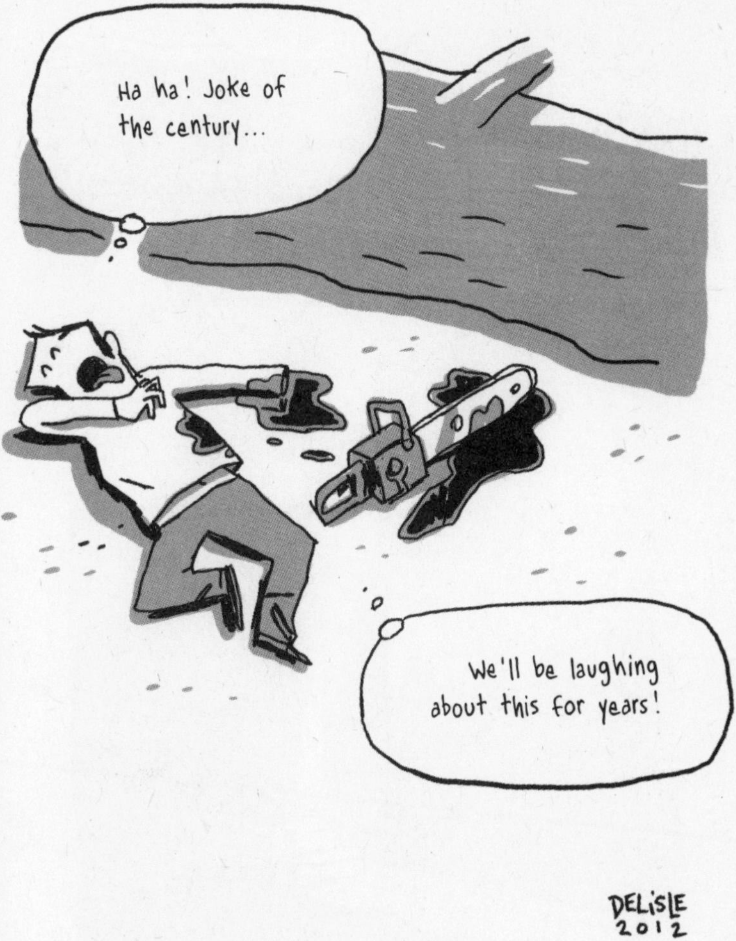
Ha ha! Joke of the century...
We'll be laughing about this for years!
DELISLE 2012

-The Easter Bunny

Dad?

Hmm?

Who hides the Easter eggs in the garden? Is it the Easter bunny or the flying bells?

The flying bells?

What are you talking about?

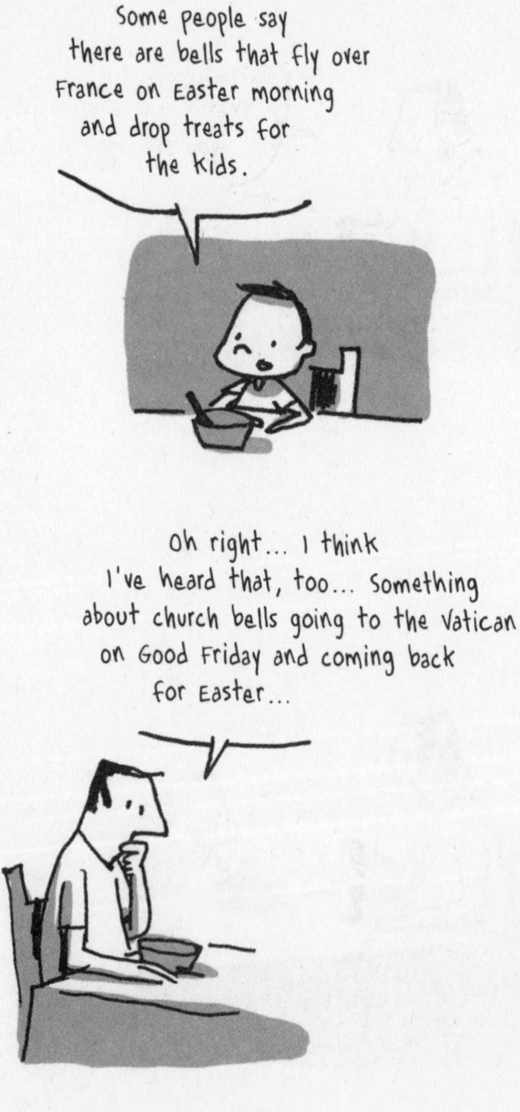
Some people say there are bells that fly over France on Easter morning and drop treats for the kids.
Oh right... I think I've heard that, too... Something about church bells going to the Vatican on Good Friday and coming back for Easter...

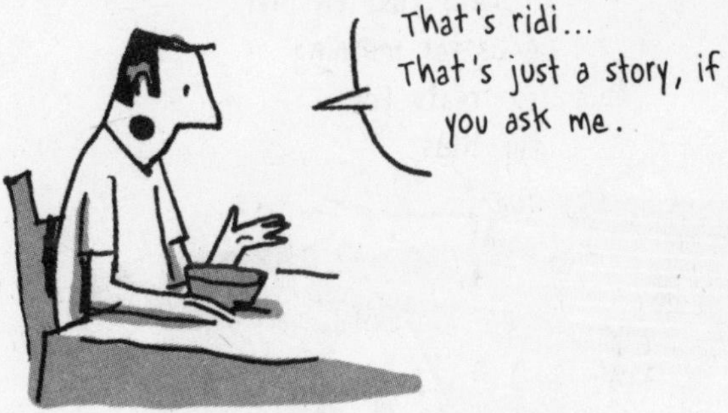
That's ridi...
That's just a story, if you ask me.

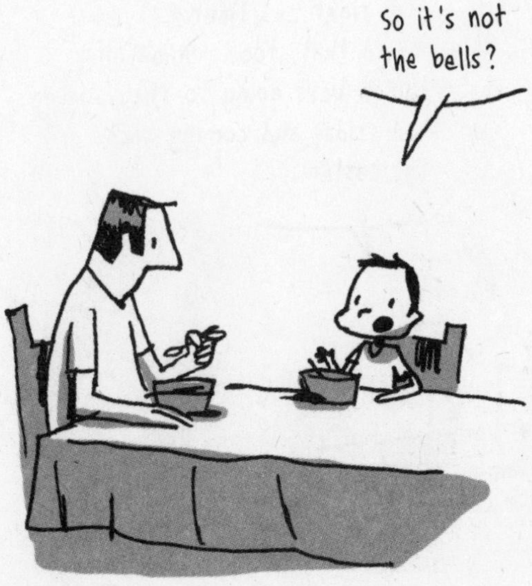
So it's not the bells?

No, of course not!

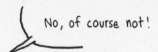

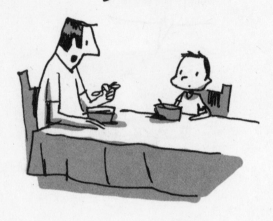

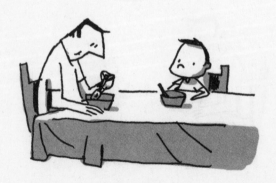

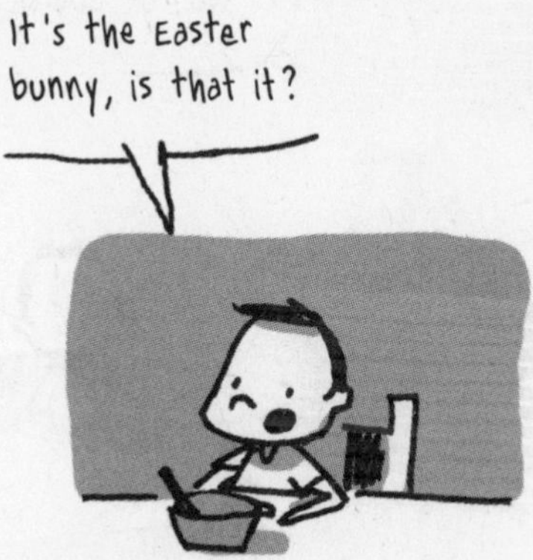
It's the Easter bunny, is that it?

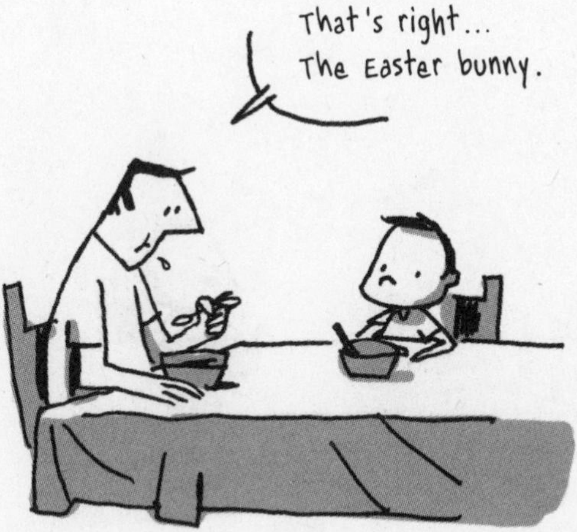
That's right... The Easter bunny.

But how does the
bunny manage to carry
the chocolate?

You're the
one hiding the
eggs, aren't
you?

Of course not...
Are you kidding?
It's a big bunny.

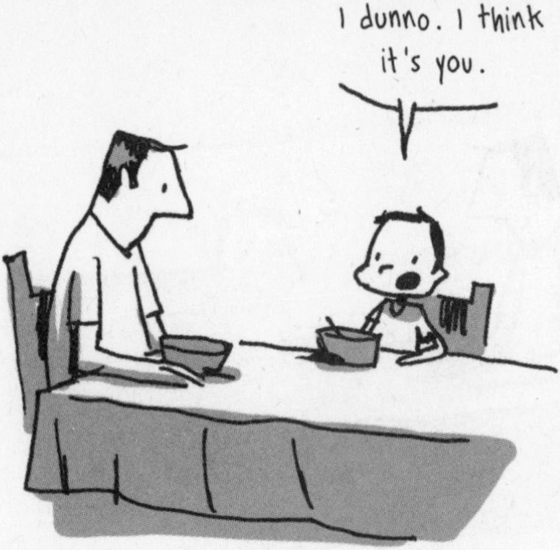
I dunno. I think it's you.

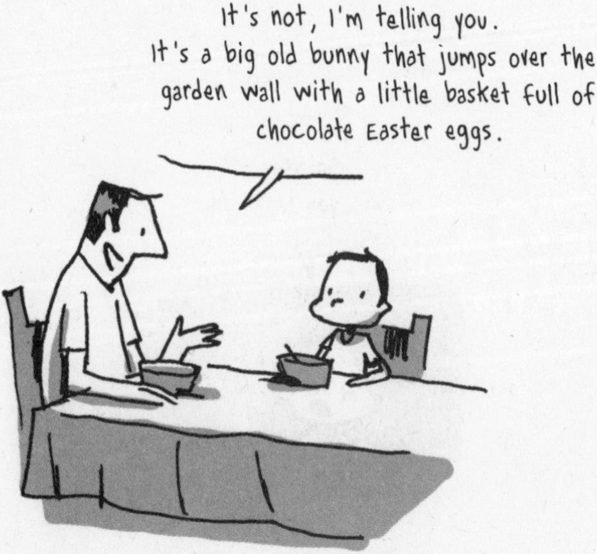
It's not, I'm telling you. It's a big old bunny that jumps over the garden wall with a little basket full of chocolate Easter eggs.

So why are
you laughing?

I'm not laughing
Not at all.
I'm taking this bunny question very seriously.

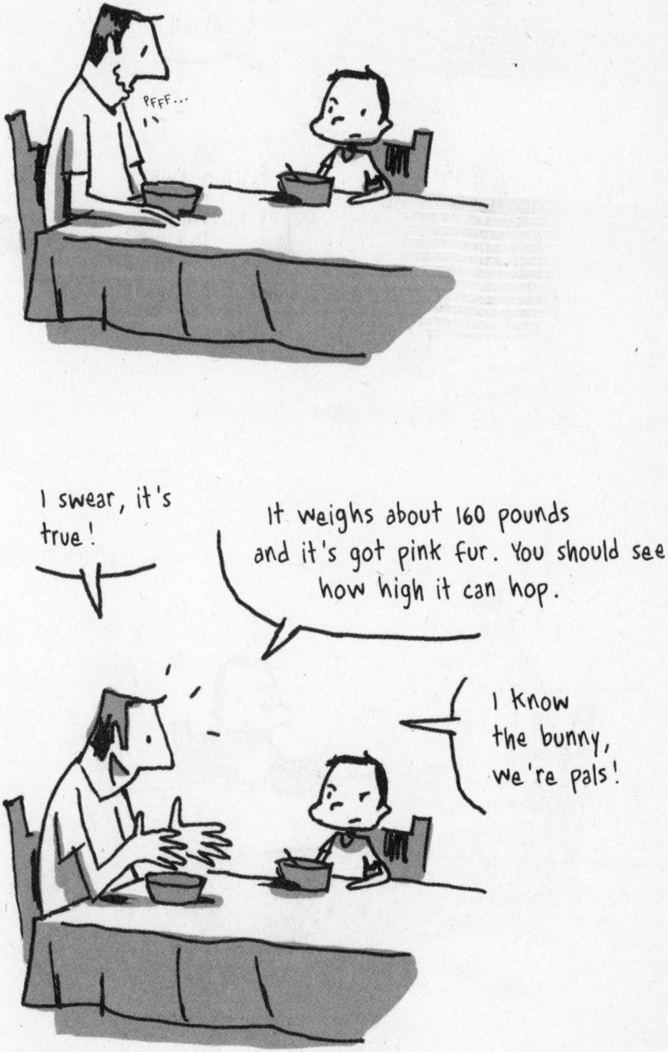
PFFF...
I swear, it's true!
It weighs about 160 pounds and it's got pink fur. You should see how high it can hop.
I know the bunny, we're pals!

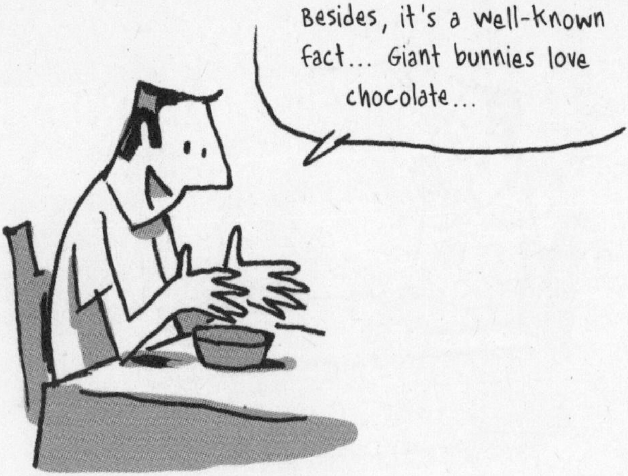
Besides, it's a well-known fact... Giant bunnies love chocolate...

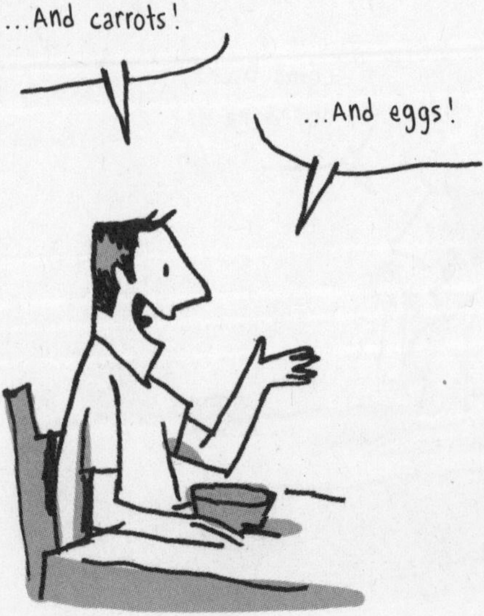
...And carrots!
...And eggs!

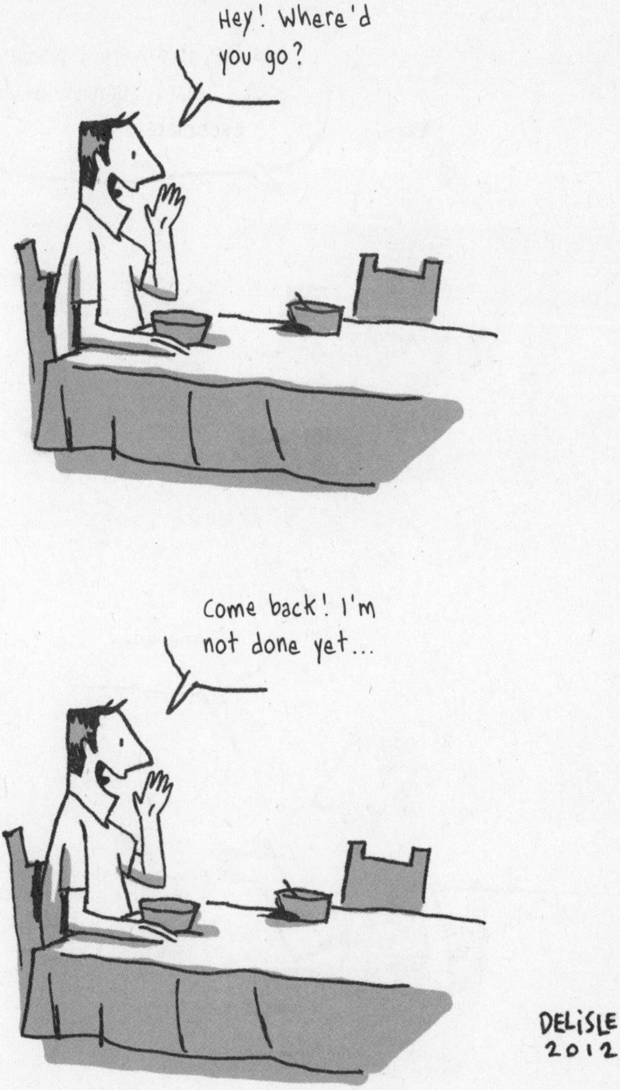
Hey! Where'd you go?
Come back! I'm not done yet...
DELISLE 2012

-The Pool

I don't wanna go.
I hate swimming!

C'mon!

You're just saying
that because your swim
teacher was a bit hard
on you last time.

But you'll pay attention this time and everything will be fine.

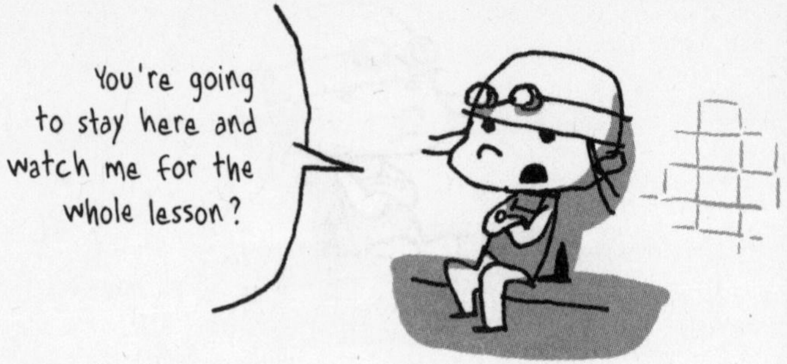
You're going to stay here and watch me for the whole lesson?

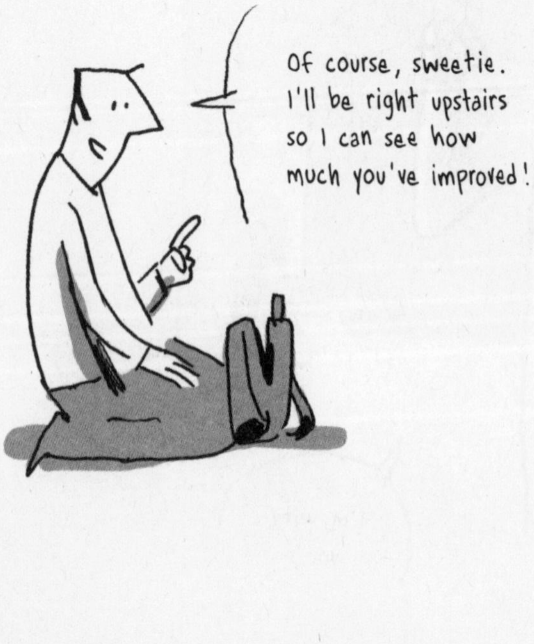
Of course, sweetie. I'll be right upstairs so I can see how much you've improved!

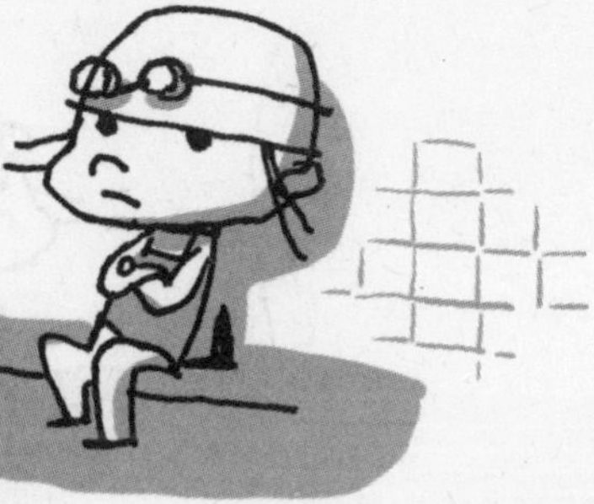

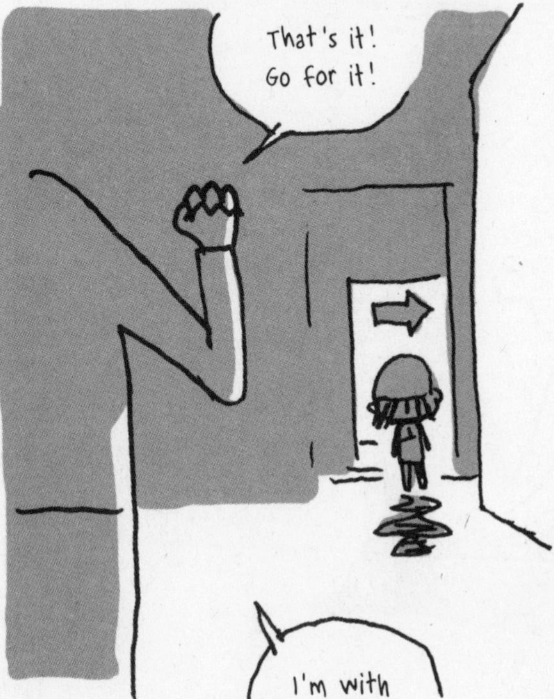
That's it!
Go for it!
I'm with
you!

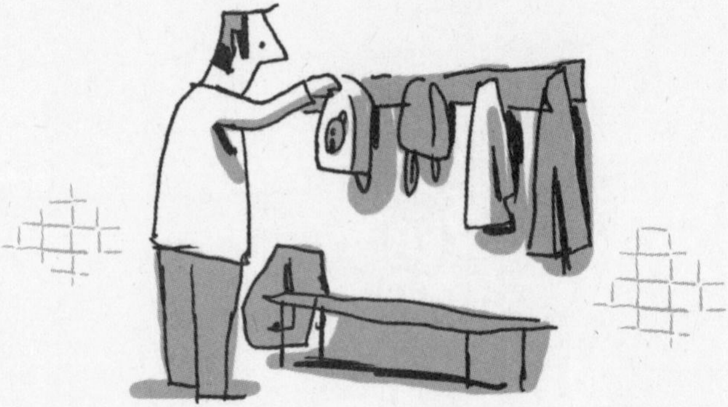

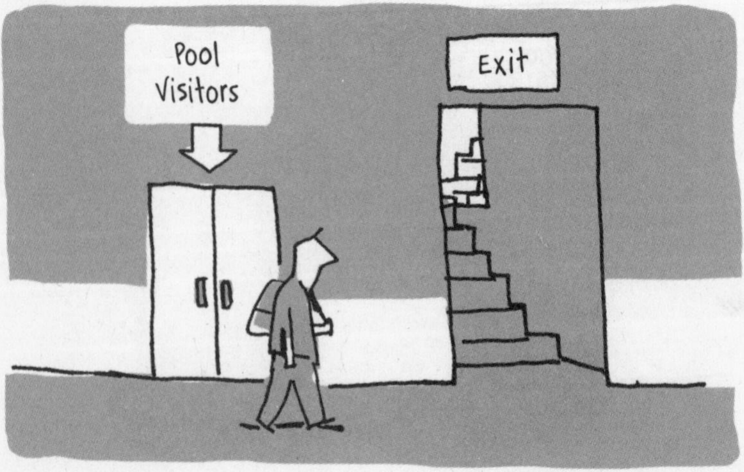
Pool
Visitors
Exit

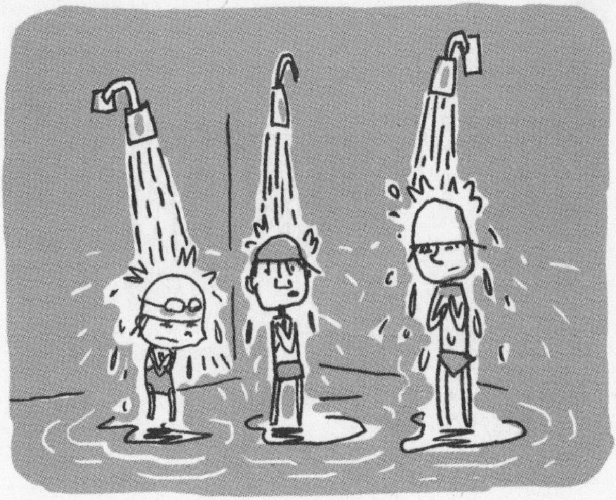

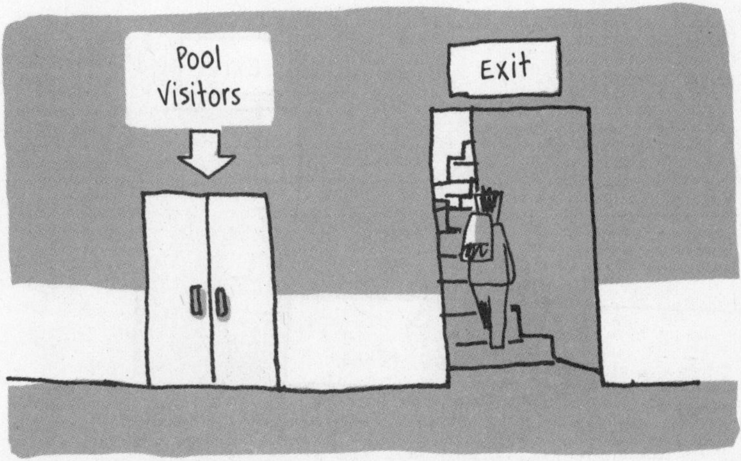
Pool
Visitors
Exit

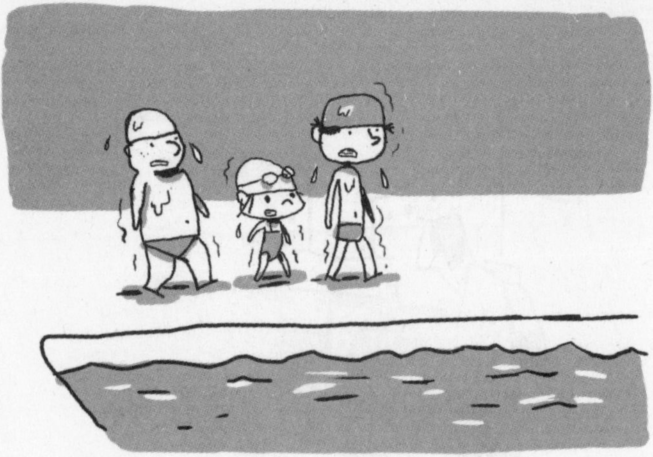

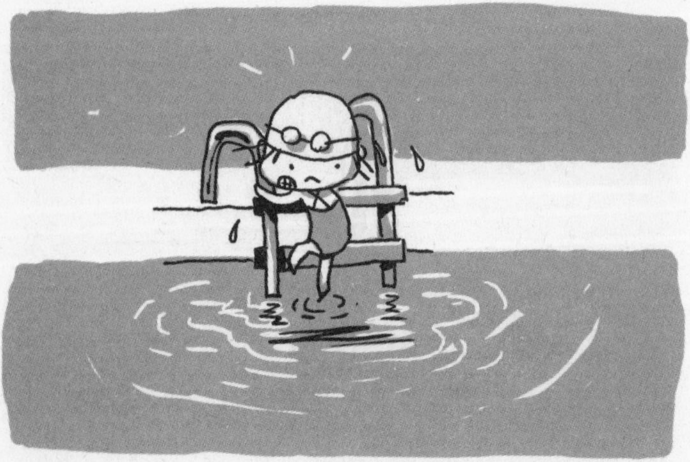

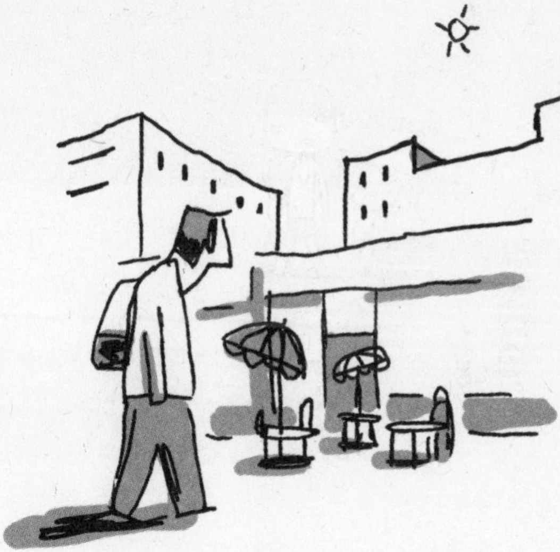

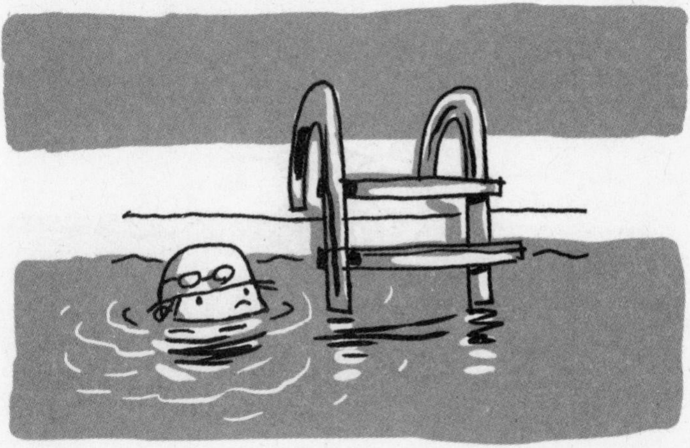

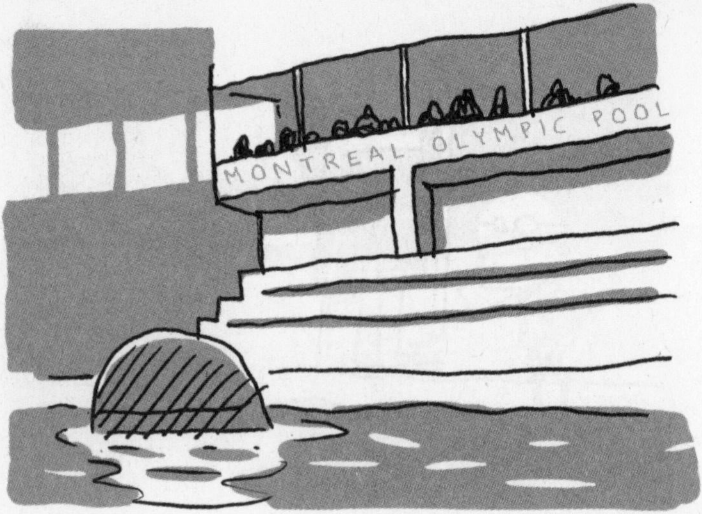
MONTREAL OLYMPIC POOL

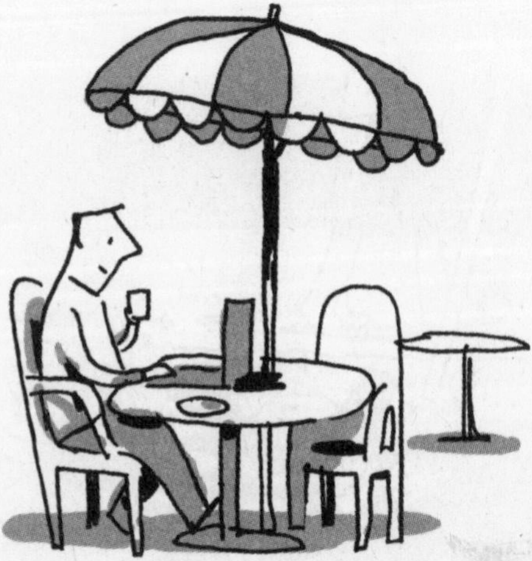

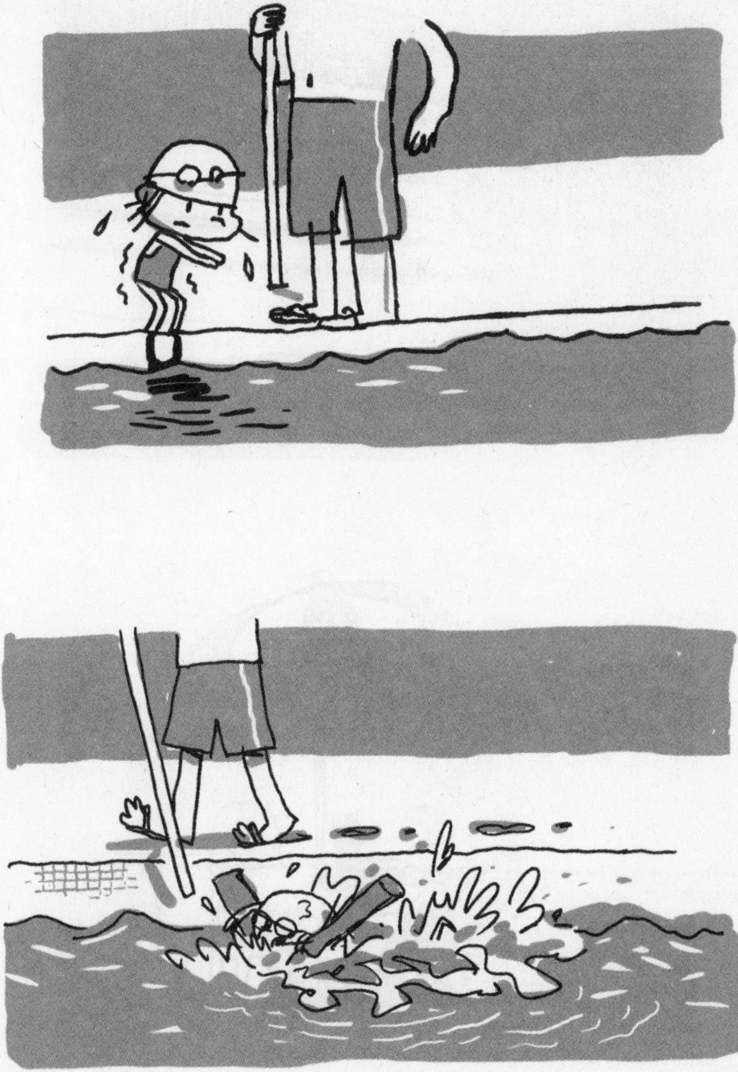

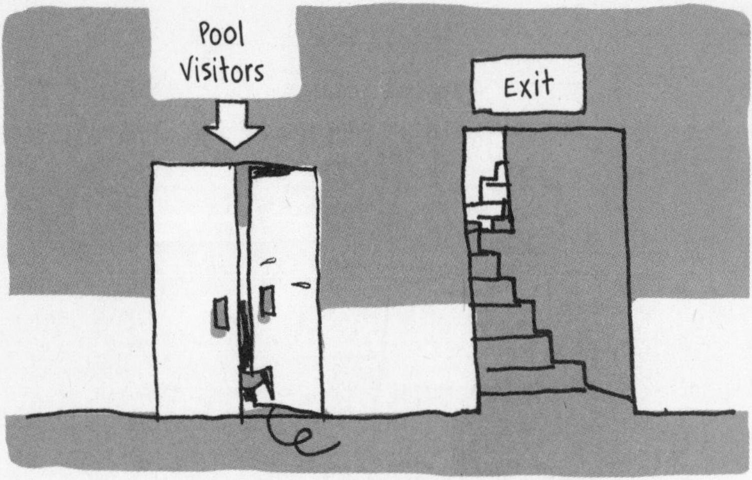
Pool
Visitors
Exit

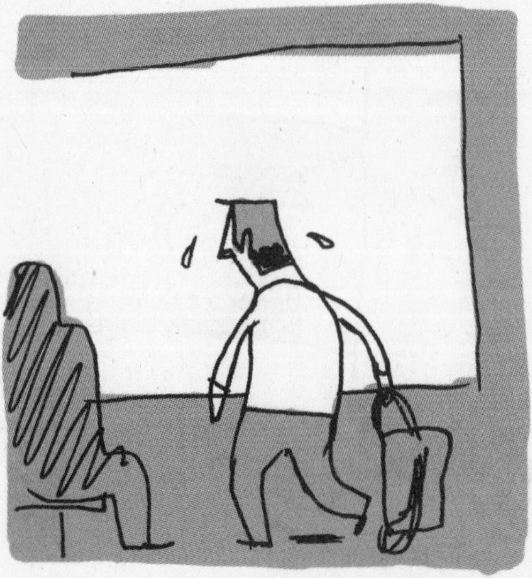

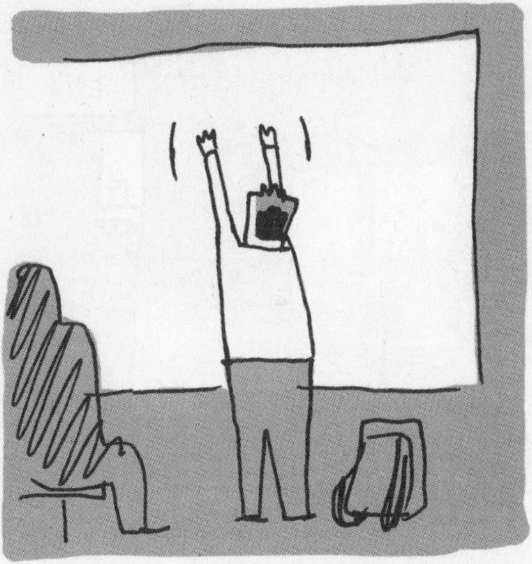

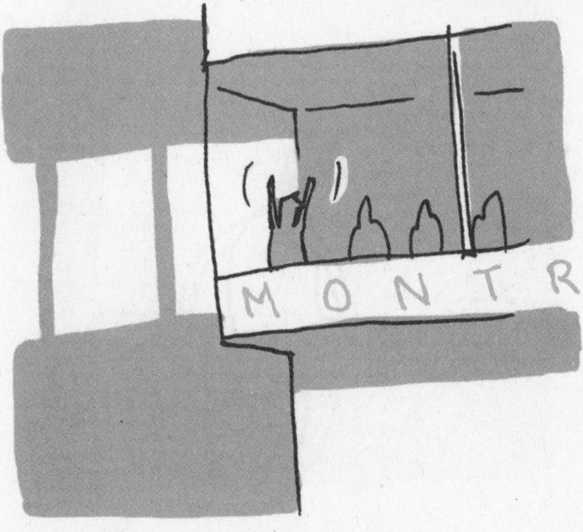
M O N T R

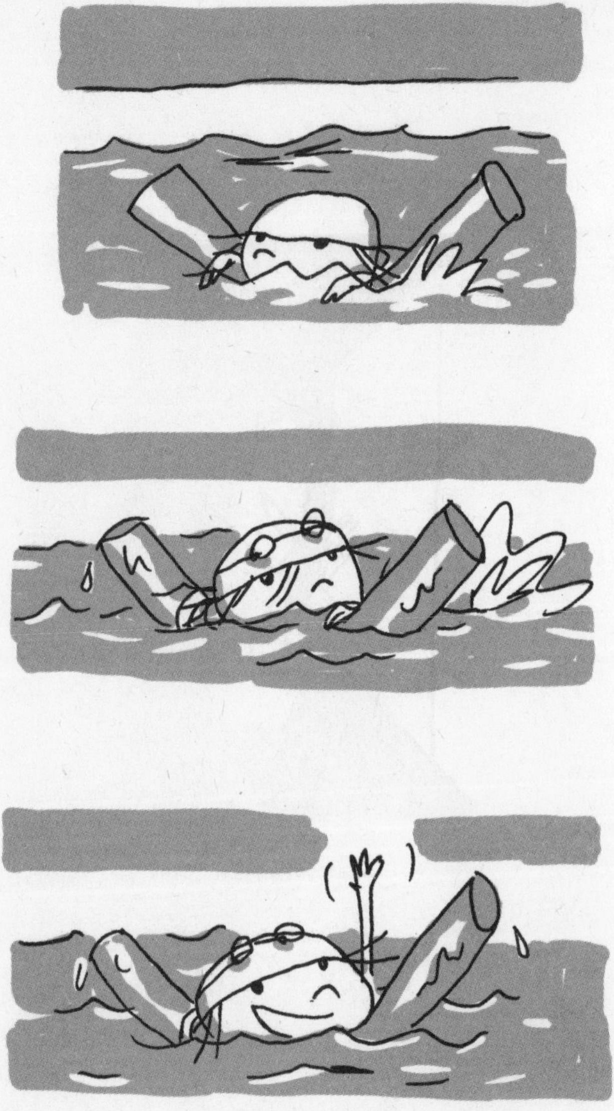

DELiSLE
2012

-The Internet

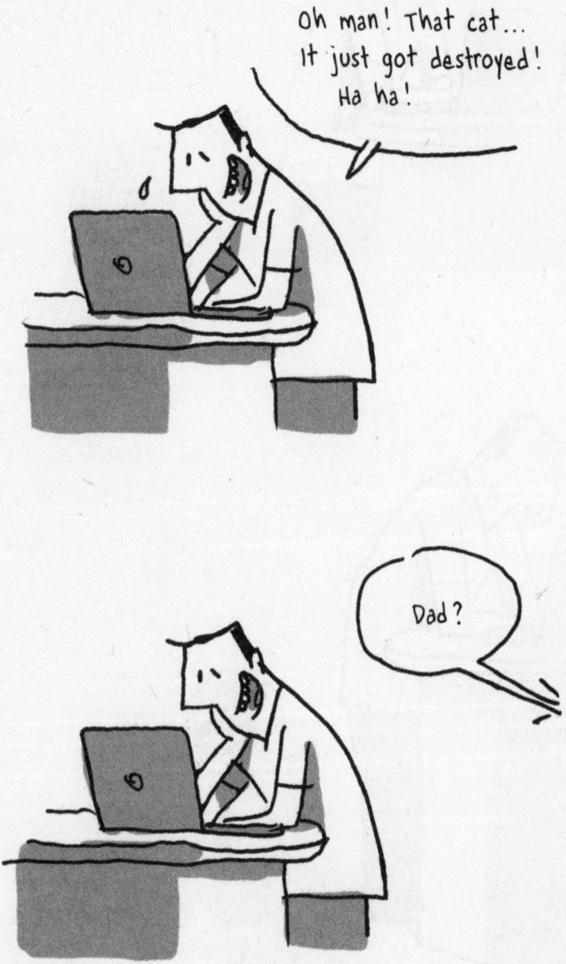
Oh man! That cat...
It just got destroyed!
Ha ha!
Dad?

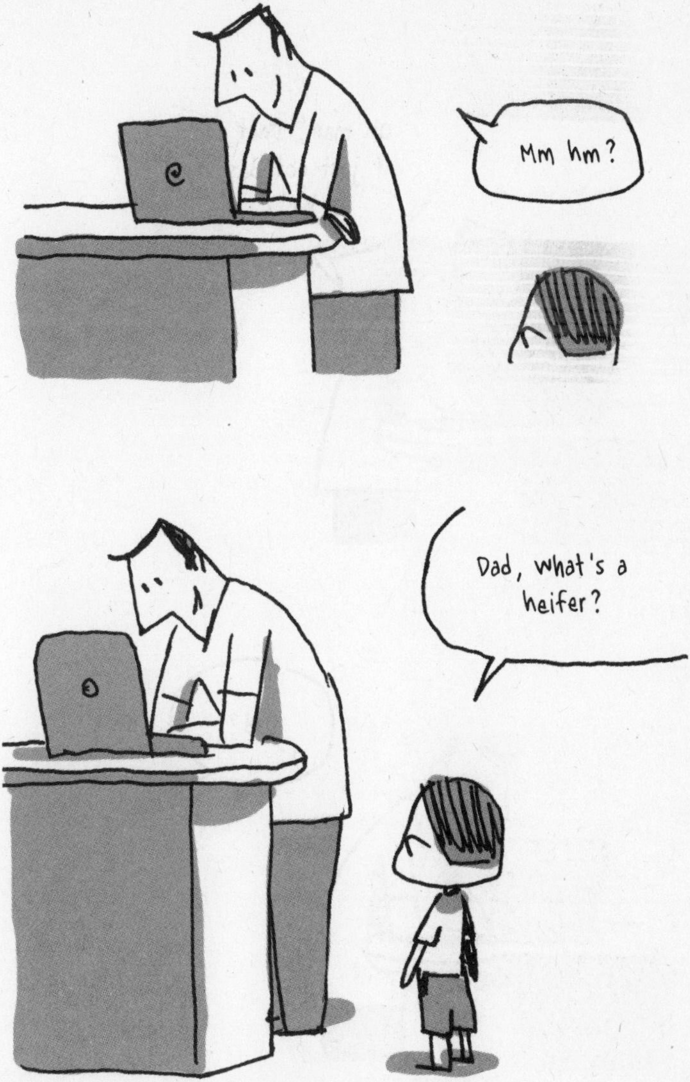
Mm hm?
Dad, what's a heifer?

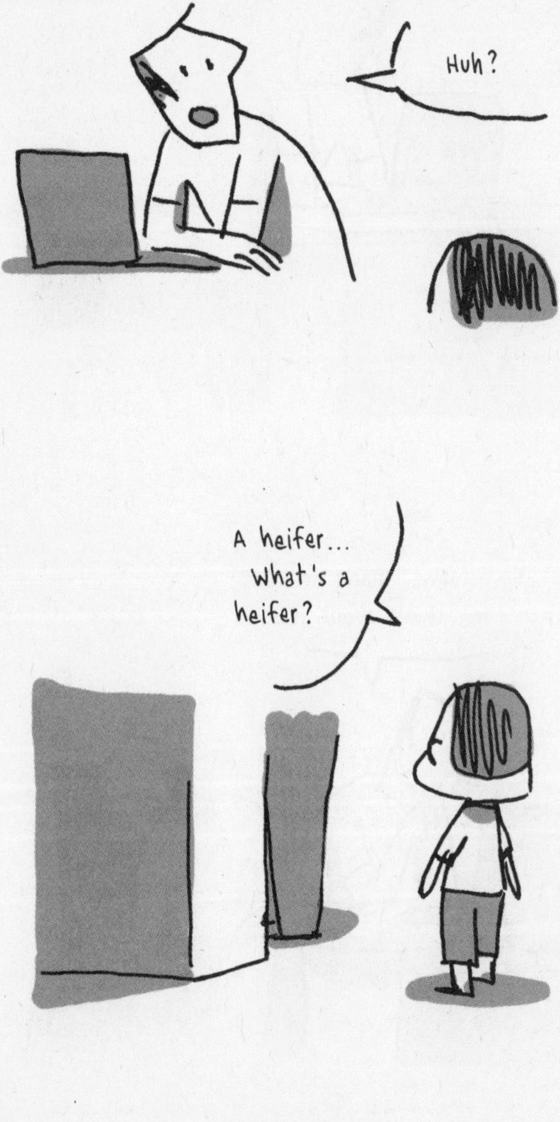
Huh?
A heifer... What's a heifer?

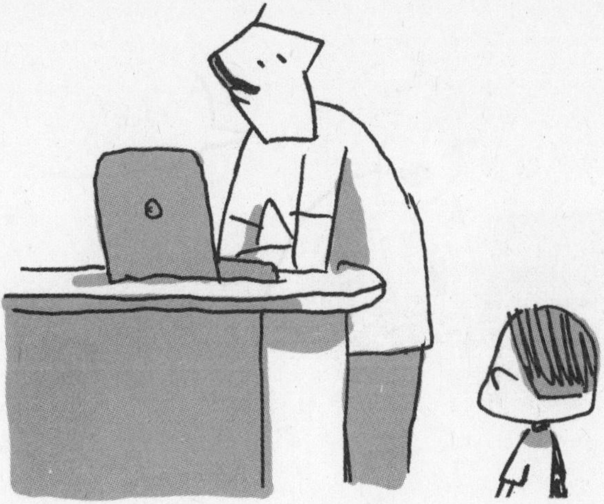

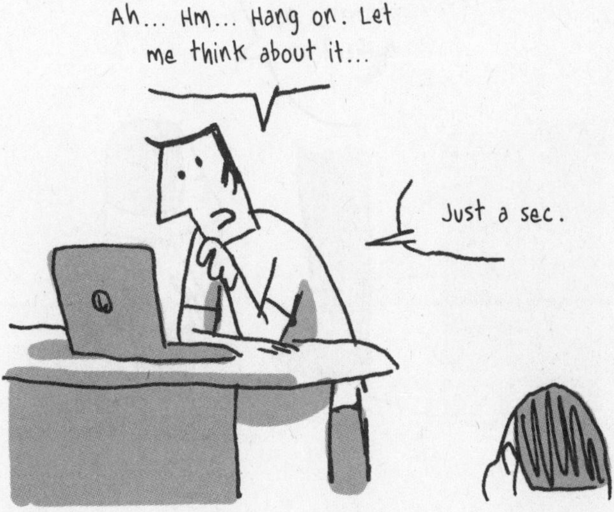
Ah... Hm... Hang on. Let me think about it...
Just a sec.

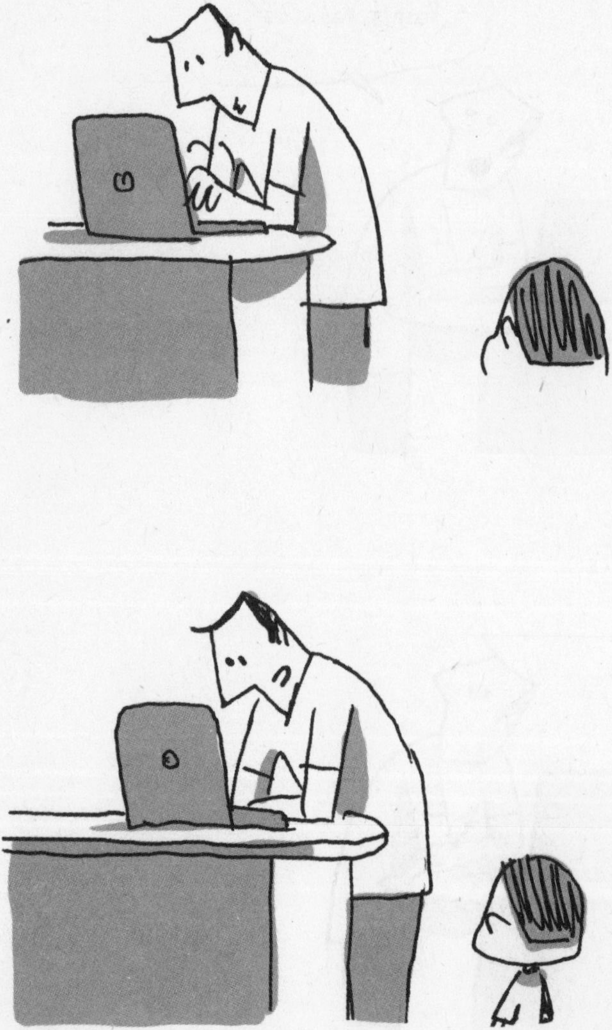

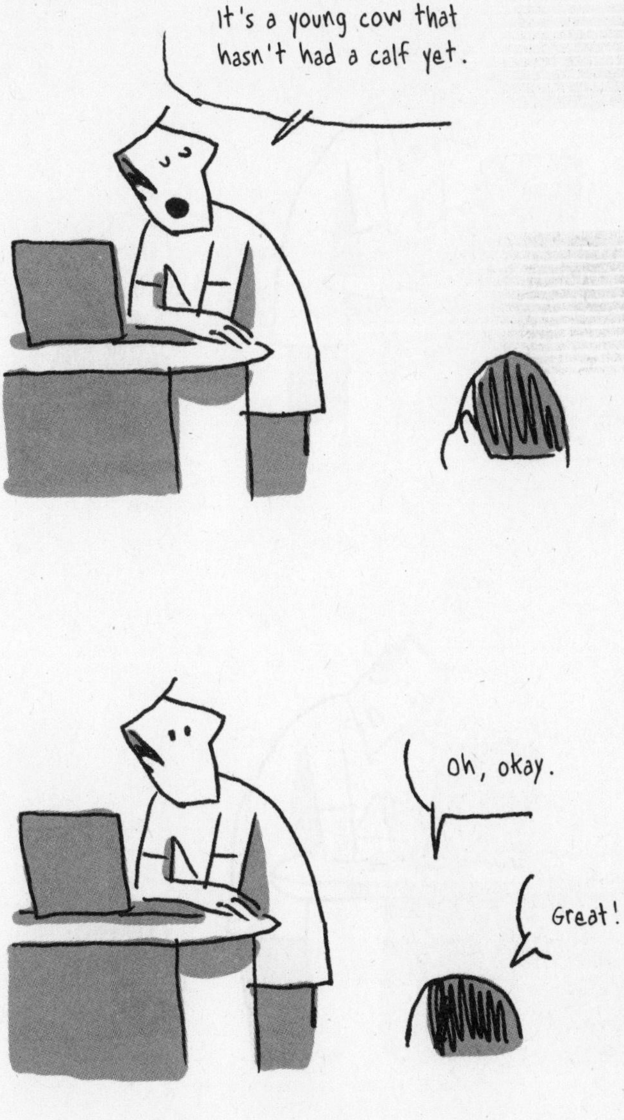
It's a young cow that hasn't had a calf yet.
Oh, okay.
Great!

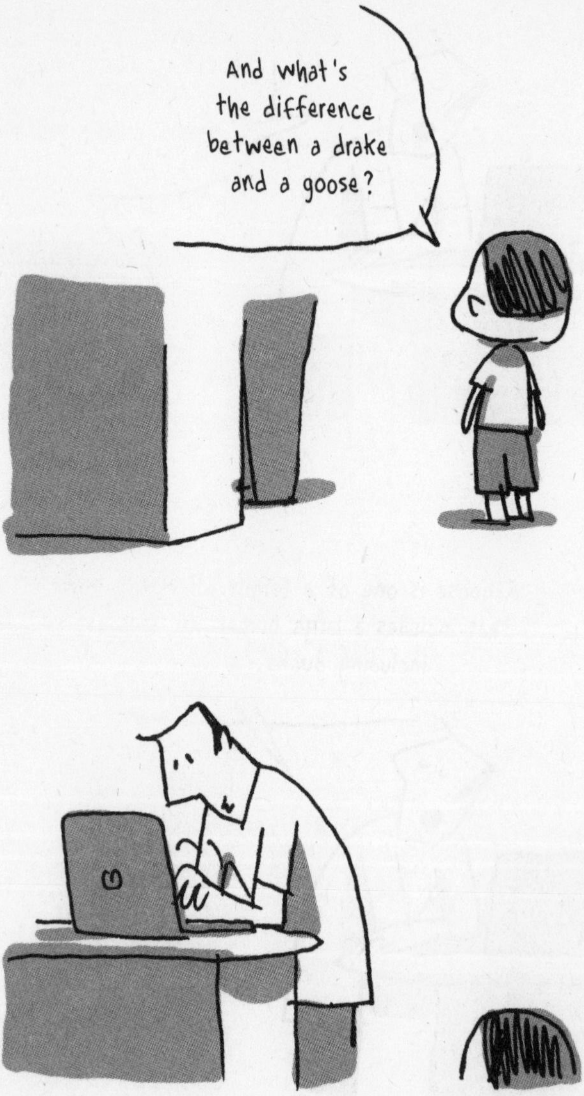
And what's the difference between a drake and a goose?

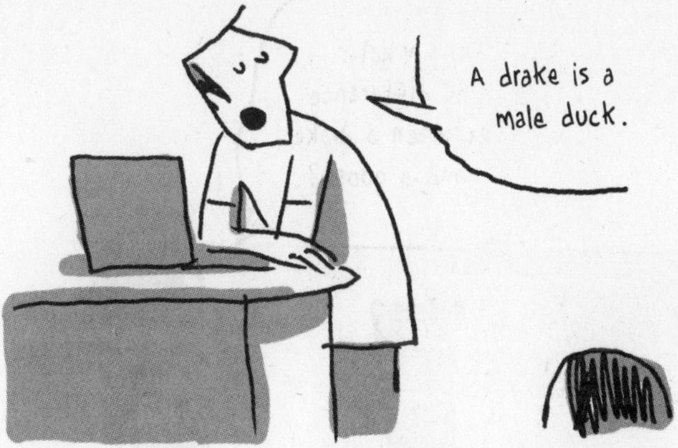
A drake is a male duck.

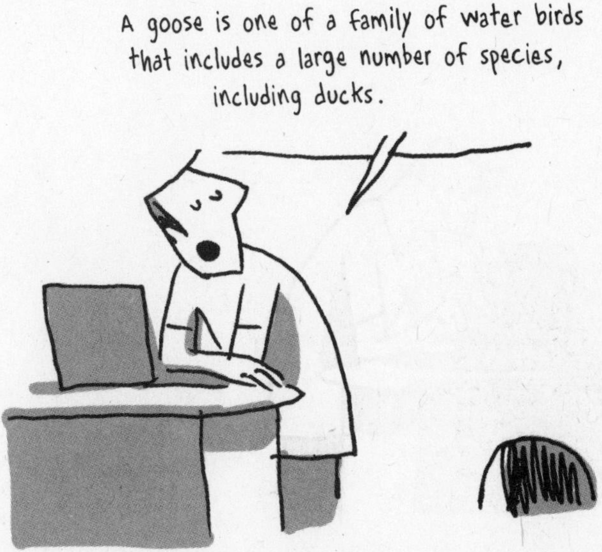
A goose is one of a family of water birds that includes a large number of species, including ducks.

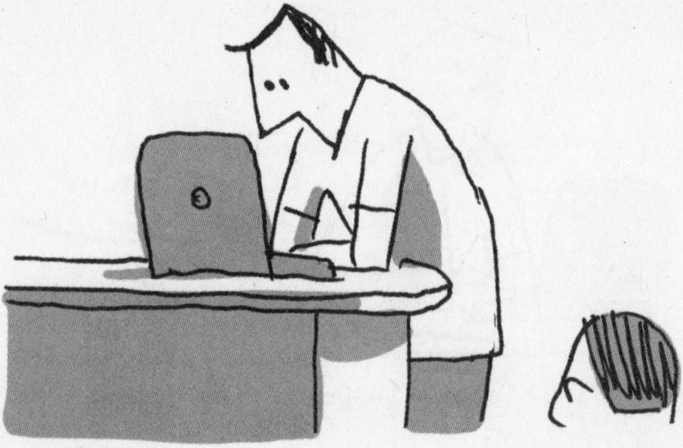

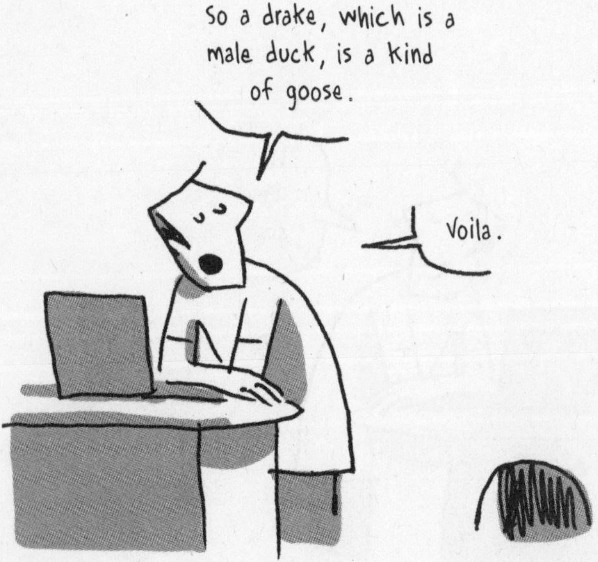
So a drake, which is a male duck, is a kind of goose.
Voila.

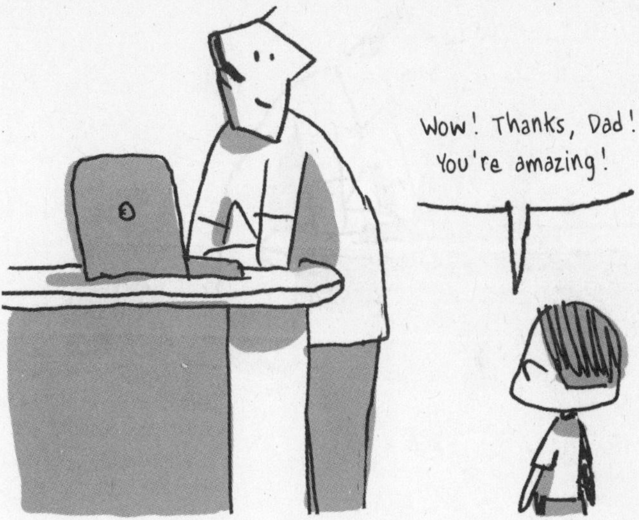
Wow! Thanks, Dad! You're amazing!

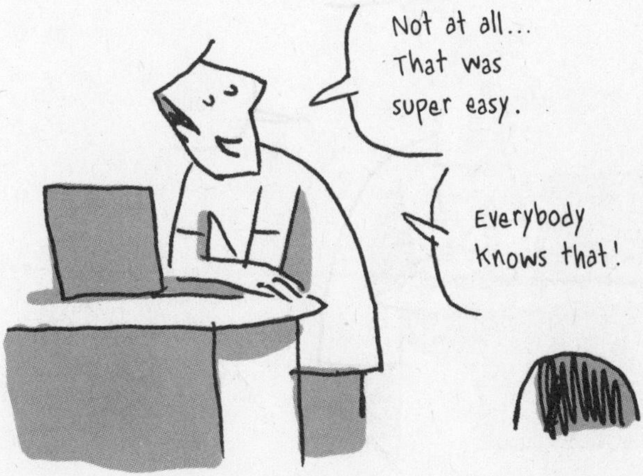
Not at all... That was super easy.
Everybody knows that!

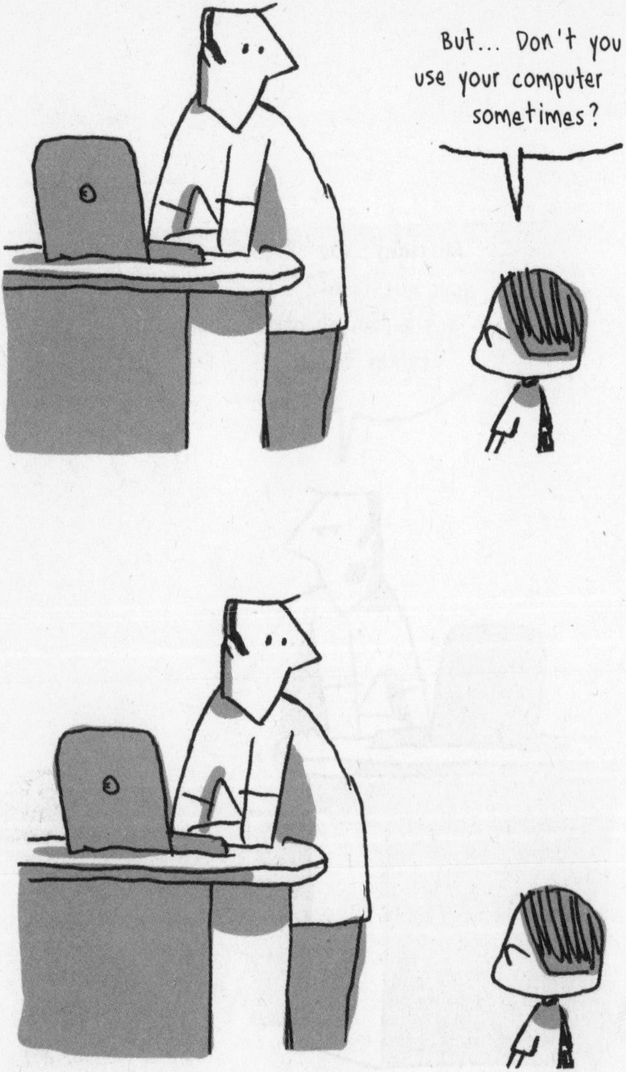
But... Don't you use your computer sometimes?

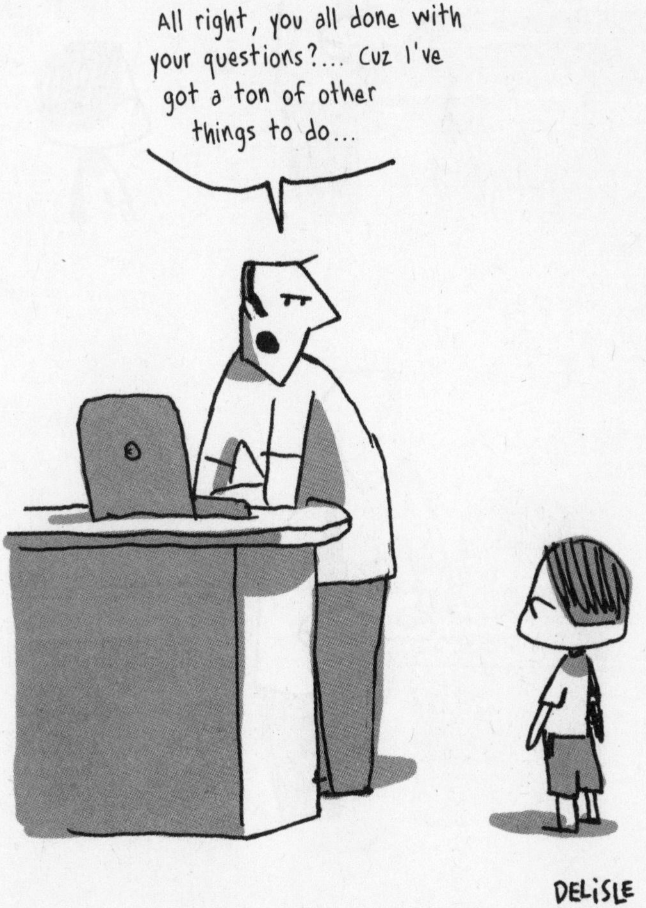
All right, you all done with your questions?... Cuz I've got a ton of other things to do...
DELISLE 2012

-The Pretty Picture

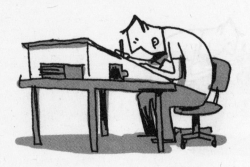

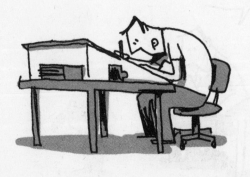

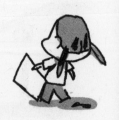

Hey, what's this?...
You brought me a
drawing?

It's beautiful!

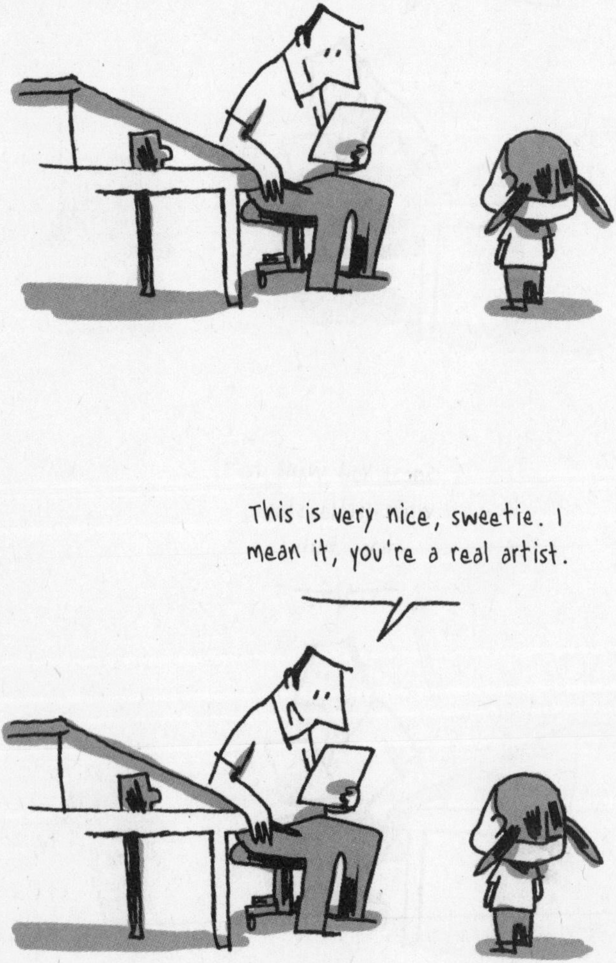
This is very nice, sweetie. I mean it, you're a real artist.

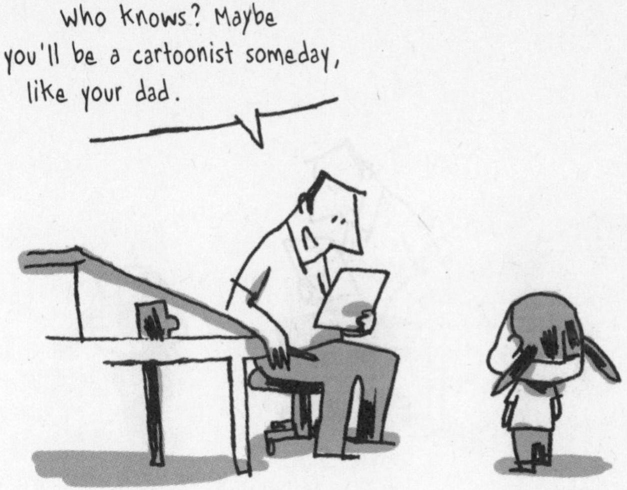
Who knows? Maybe you'll be a cartoonist someday, like your dad.

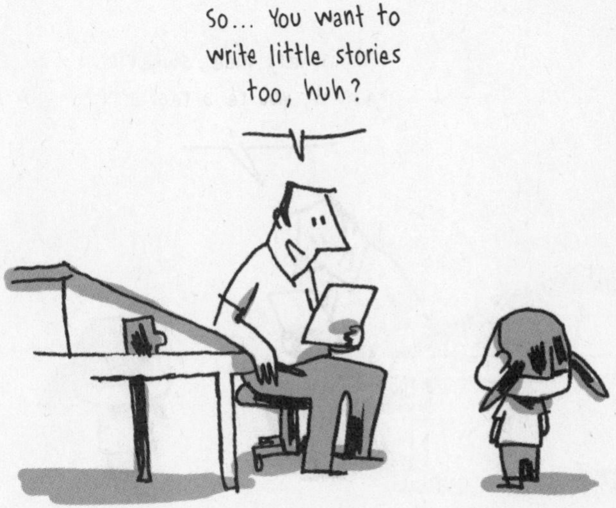
So... You want to write little stories too, huh?

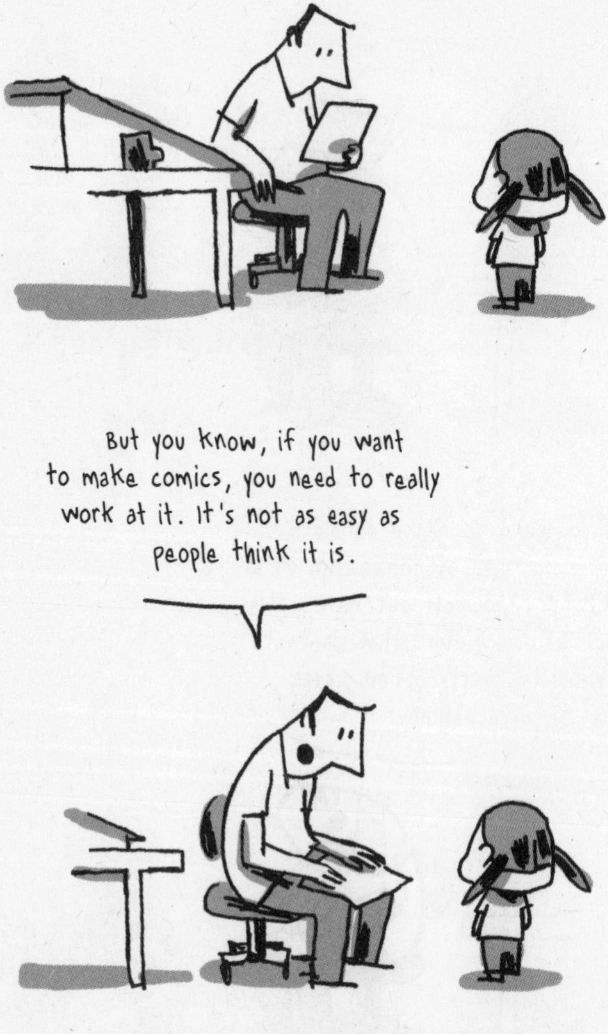
But you know, if you want to make comics, you need to really work at it. It's not as easy as people think it is.

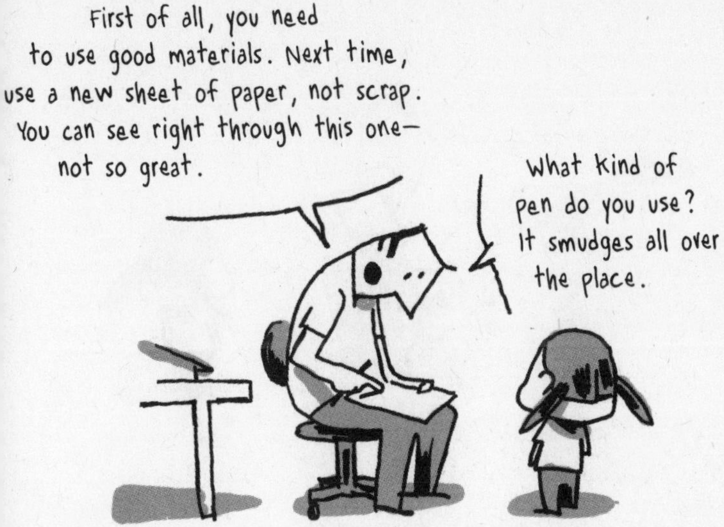
First of all, you need to use good materials. Next time, use a new sheet of paper, not scrap. You can see right through this one— not so great.
What kind of pen do you use? It smudges all over the place.

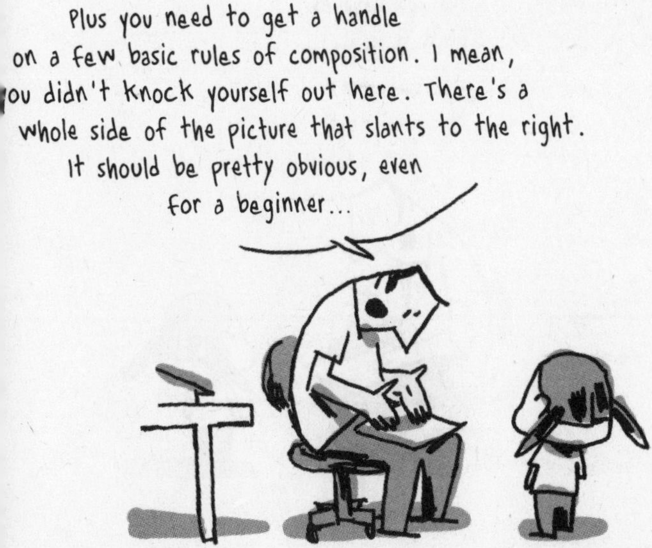
Plus you need to get a handle on a few basic rules of composition. I mean, you didn't knock yourself out here. There's a whole side of the picture that slants to the right. It should be pretty obvious, even for a beginner...

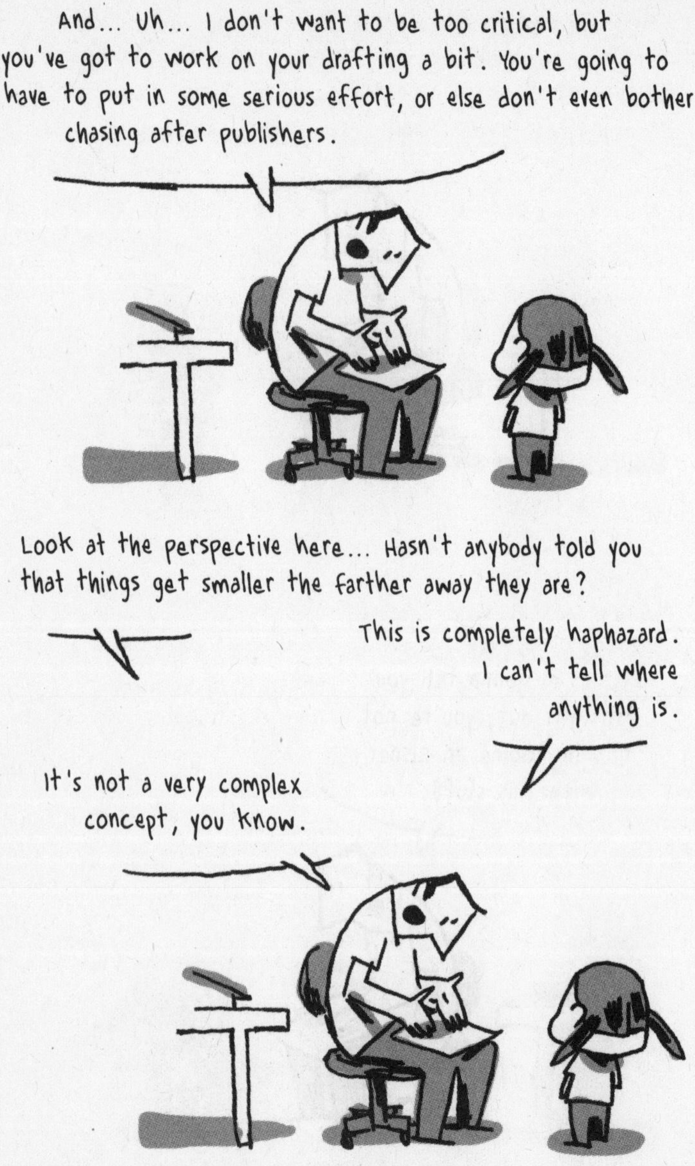
And... Uh... I don't want to be too critical, but you've got to work on your drafting a bit. You're going to have to put in some serious effort, or else don't even bother chasing after publishers.
Look at the perspective here... Hasn't anybody told you that things get smaller the farther away they are?
This is completely haphazard. I can't tell where anything is.
It's not a very complex concept, you know.

I'm gonna tell you straight out, you're not bringing home an Eisner with this stuff.

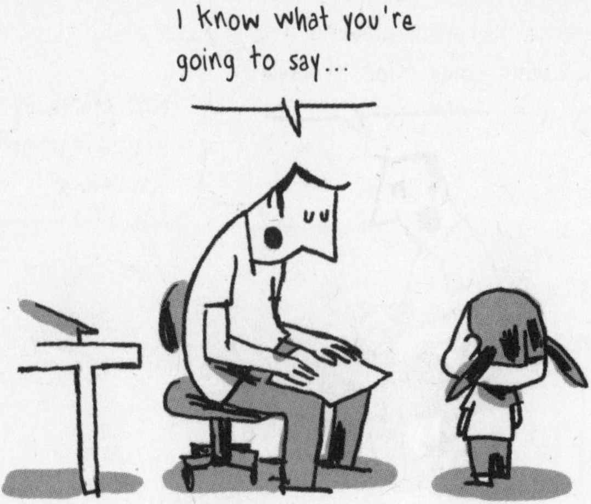
I know what you're going to say...

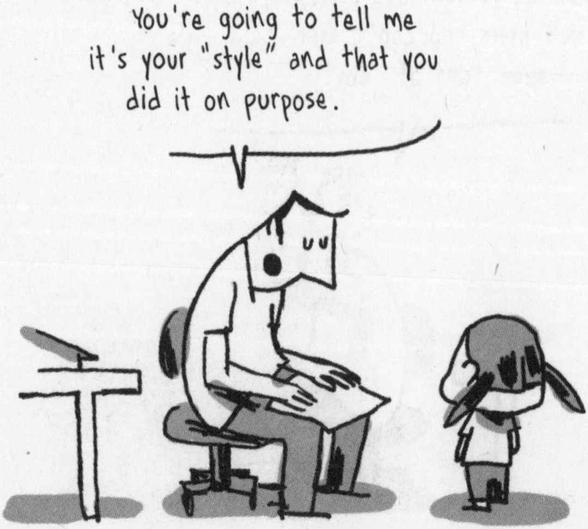
You're going to tell me it's your "style" and that you did it on purpose.

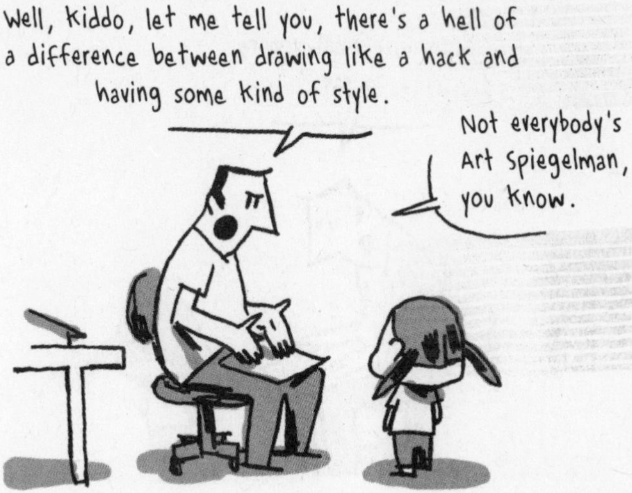
Well, kiddo, let me tell you, there's a hell of a difference between drawing like a hack and having some kind of style.
Not everybody's Art Spiegelman, you know.

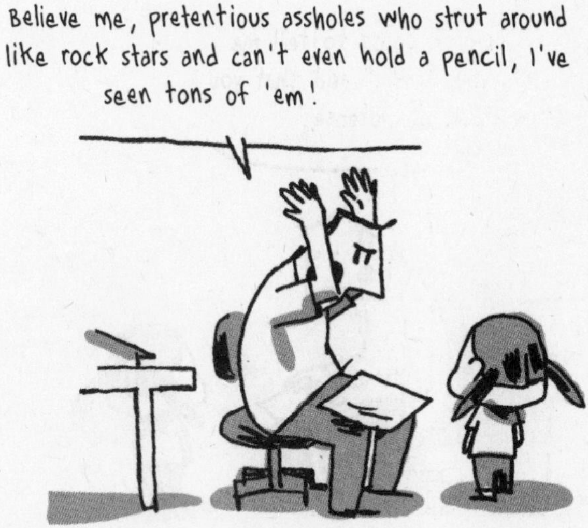
Believe me, pretentious assholes who strut around like rock stars and can't even hold a pencil, I've seen tons of 'em!

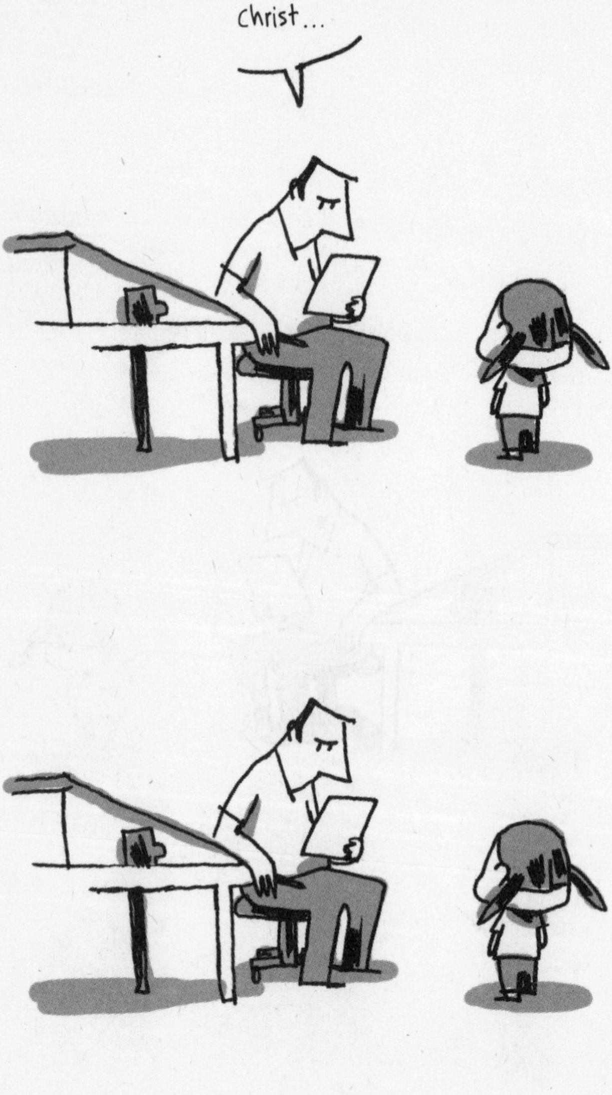
Christ...

Wankers, just a bunch of wankers.
DELISLE 2012

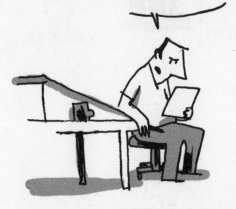

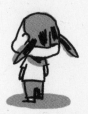

-Education

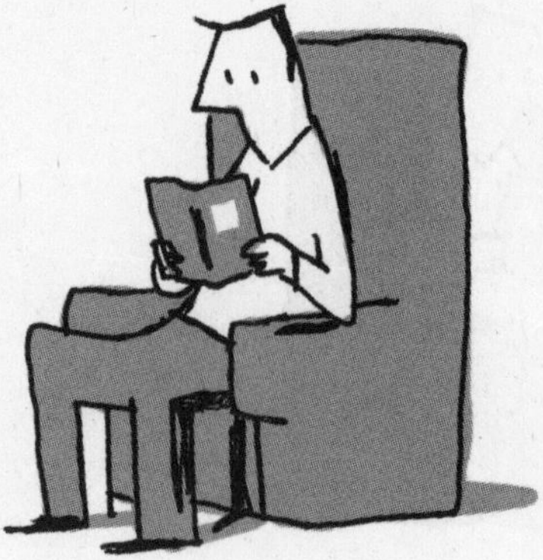

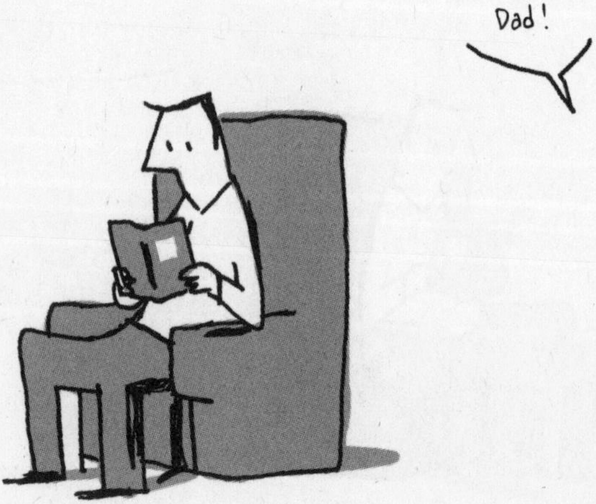
Dad!

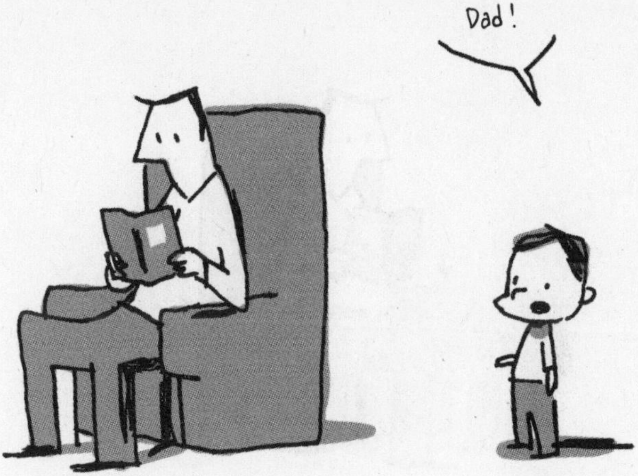
Dad!

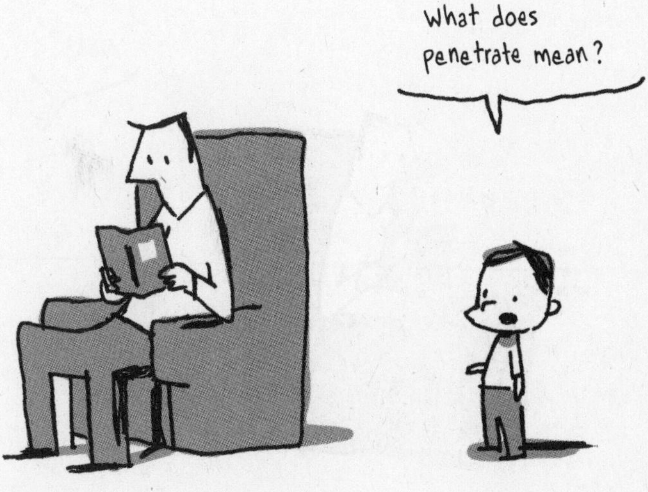
What does penetrate mean?

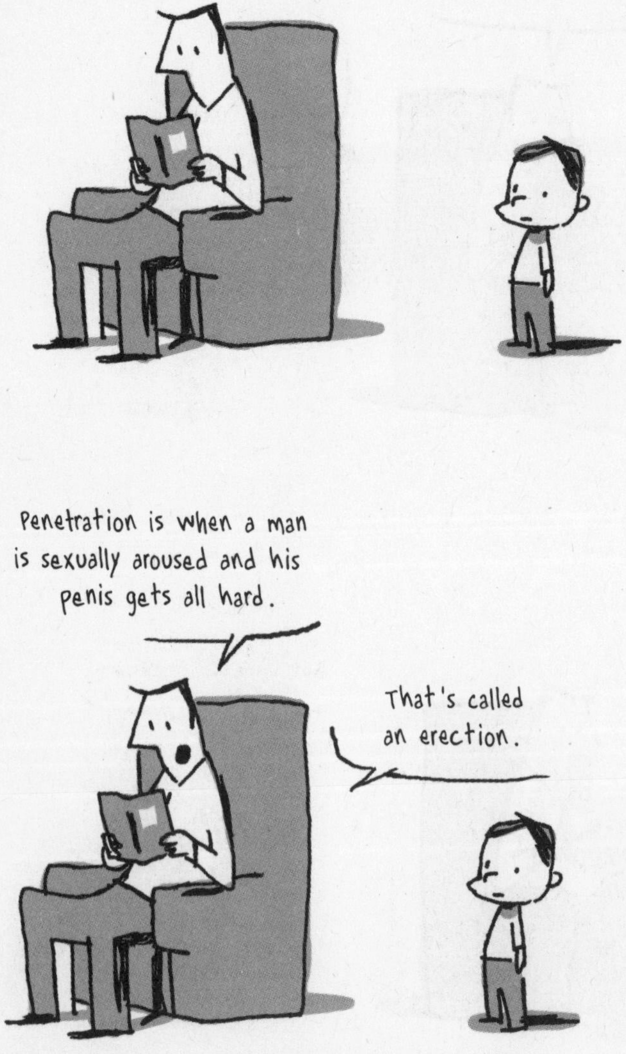
Penetration is when a man is sexually aroused and his penis gets all hard.
That's called an erection.

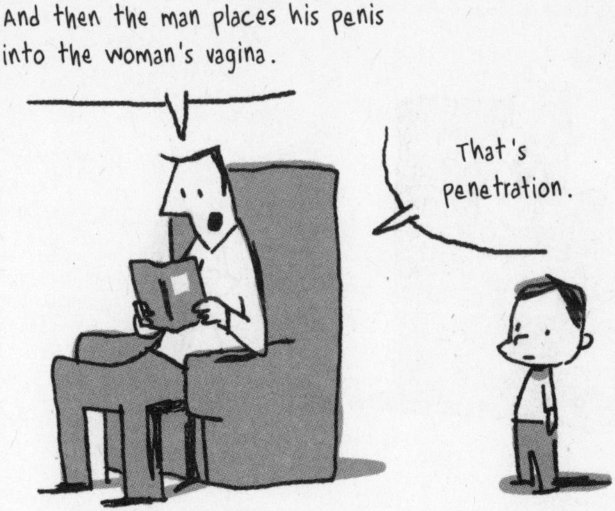
And then the man places his penis into the woman's vagina.
That's penetration.

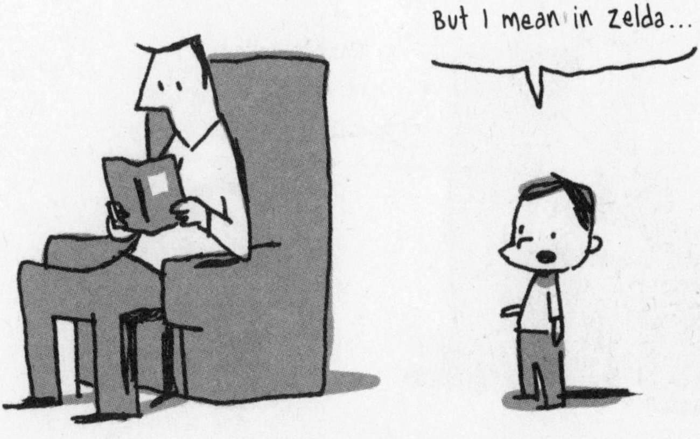
But I mean in Zelda...

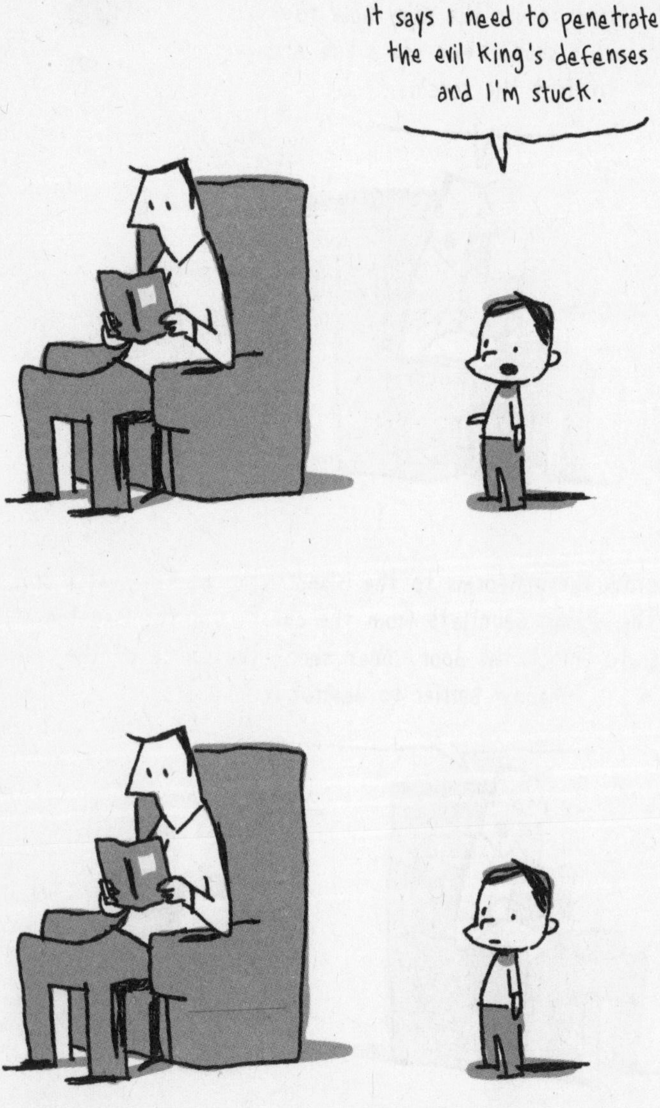
It says I need to penetrate the evil king's defenses and I'm stuck.

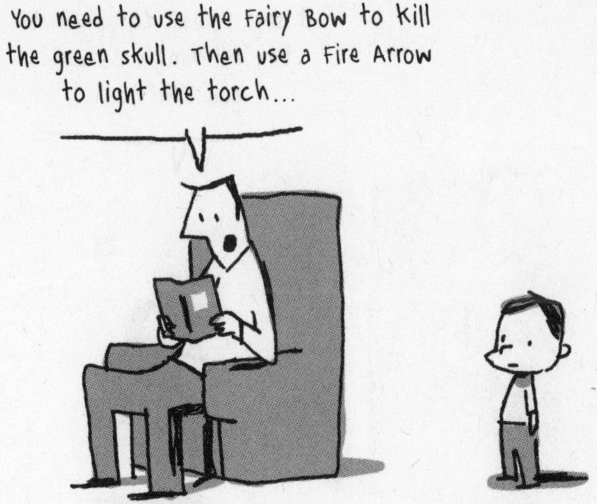
You need to use the Fairy Bow to kill the green skull. Then use a Fire Arrow to light the torch...

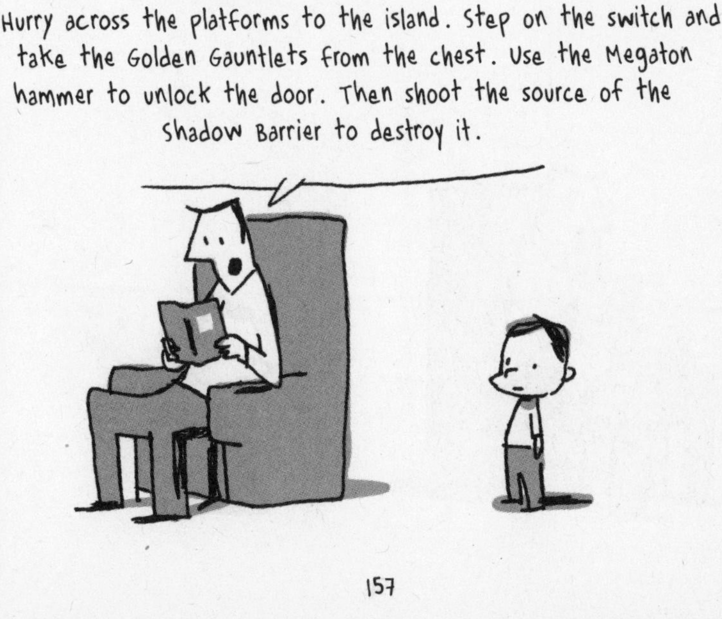
Hurry across the platforms to the island. Step on the switch and take the Golden Gauntlets from the chest. Use the Megaton hammer to unlock the door. Then shoot the source of the Shadow Barrier to destroy it.

Cool!

Thanks.

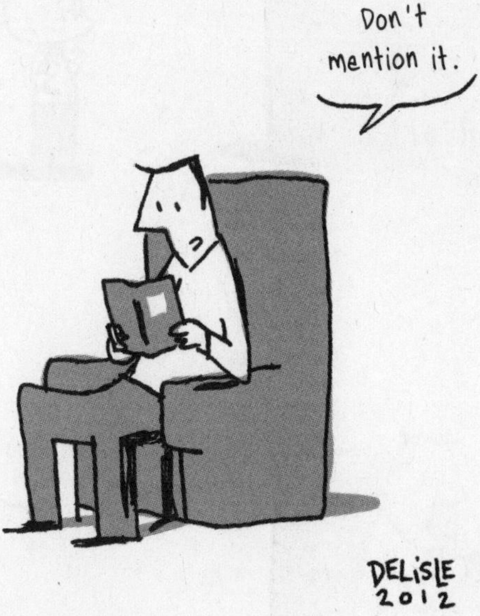
Don't mention it.
DELISLE 2012

-Cereal

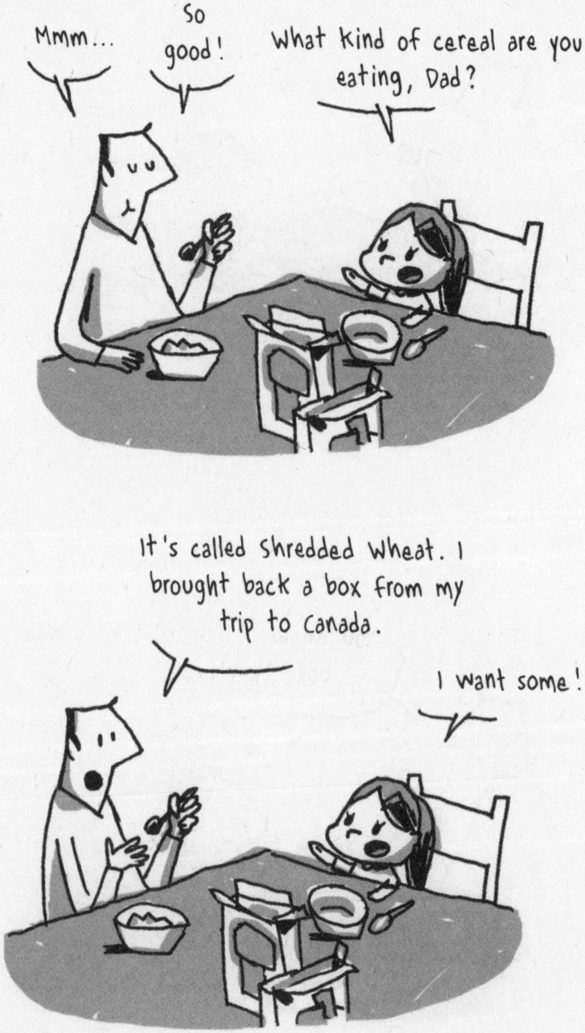
Mmm...
So good!
What kind of cereal are you eating, Dad?
It's called Shredded Wheat. I brought back a box from my trip to Canada.
I want some!

You know... I brought back <u>one</u> box, that's all.

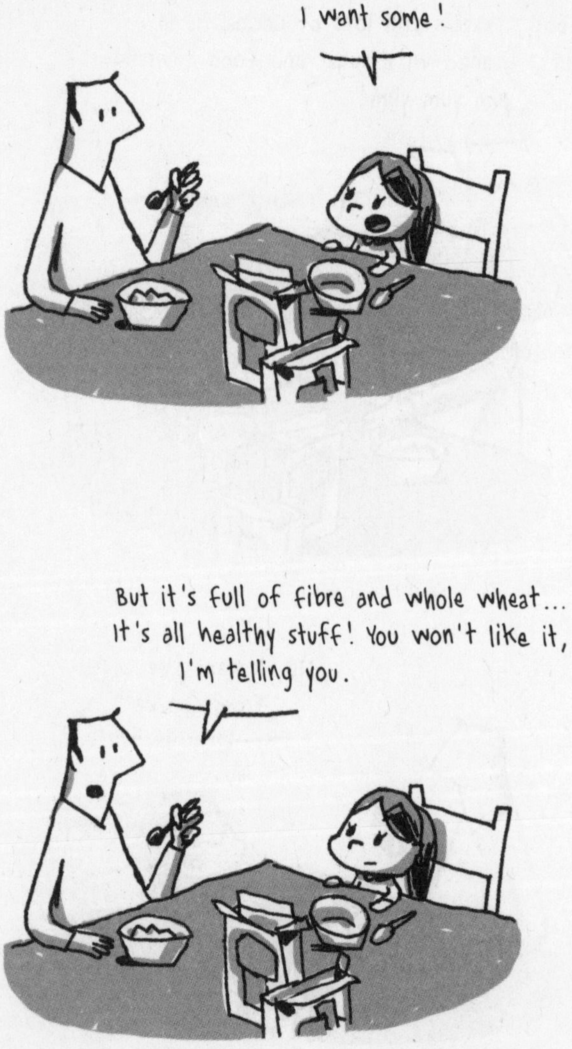
I want some!
But it's full of fibre and whole wheat... It's all healthy stuff! You won't like it, I'm telling you.

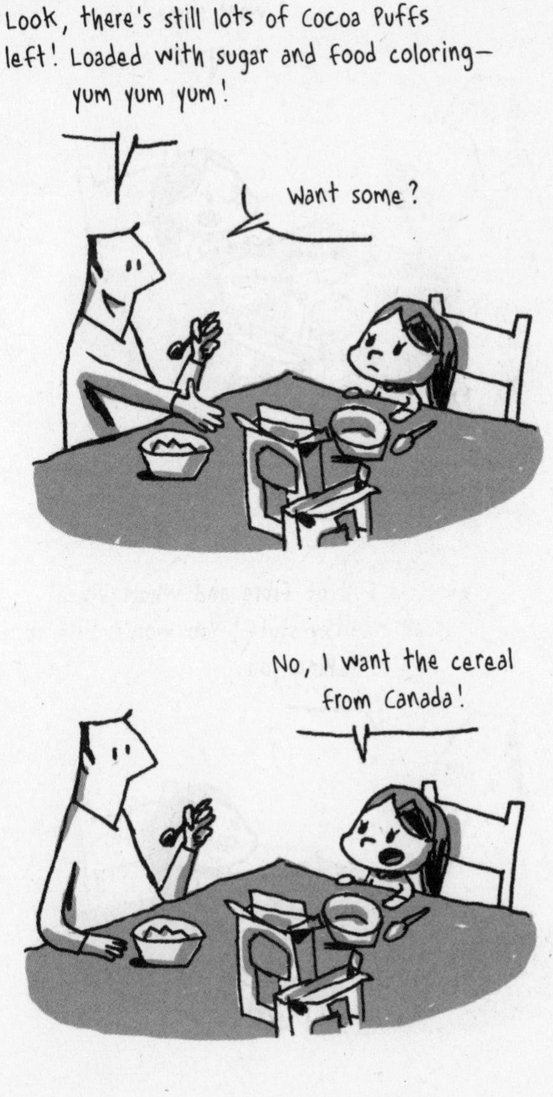
Look, there's still lots of Cocoa Puffs left! Loaded with sugar and food coloring— yum yum yum!
Want some?
No, I want the cereal from Canada!

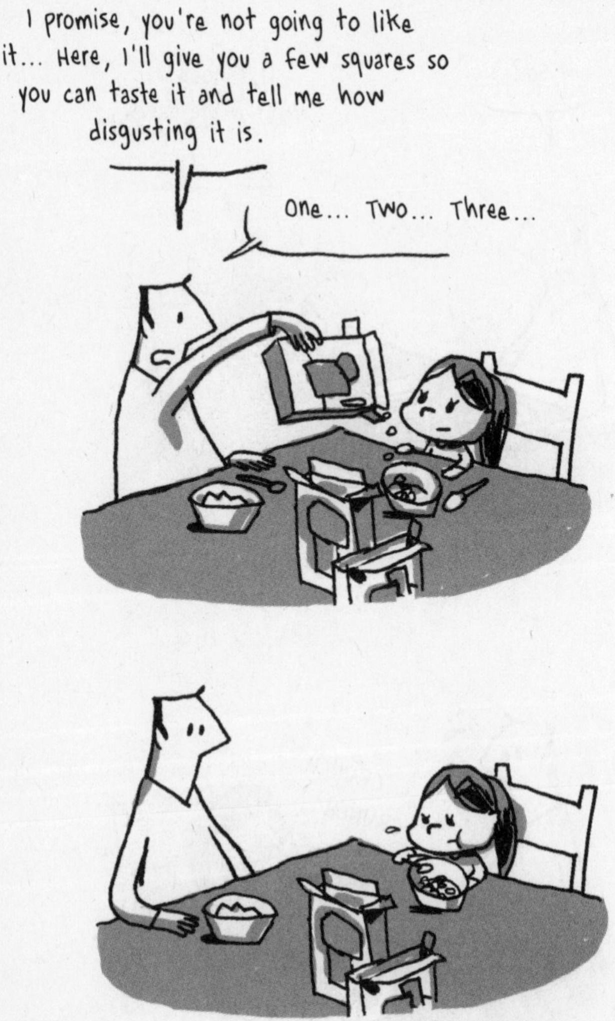
I promise, you're not going to like it... Here, I'll give you a few squares so you can taste it and tell me how disgusting it is.
One... Two... Three...

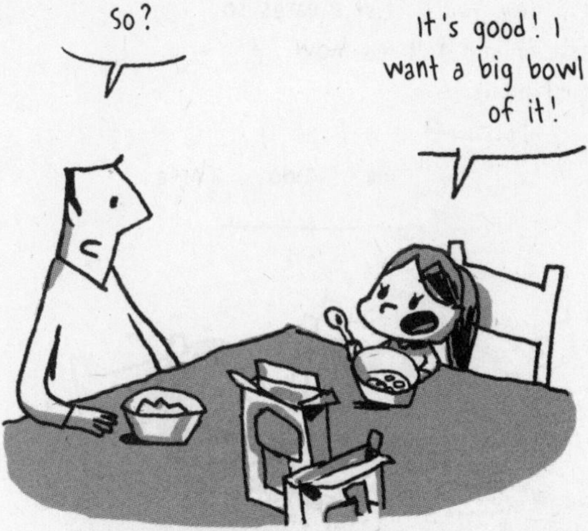
So?
It's good! I want a big bowl of it!

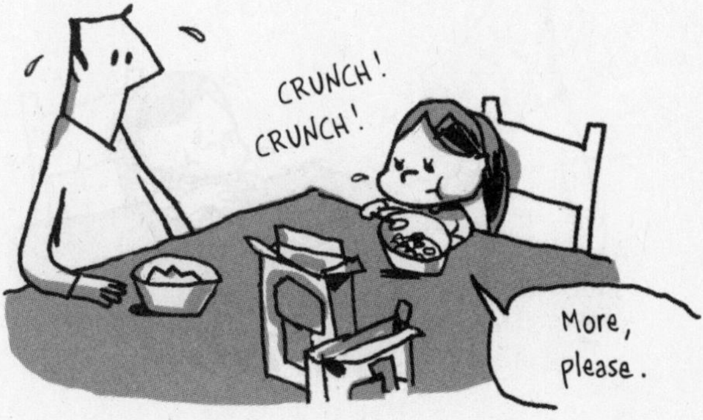
CRUNCH! CRUNCH!
More, please.

The Next Day
Can I have the new cereal?
There's none left.

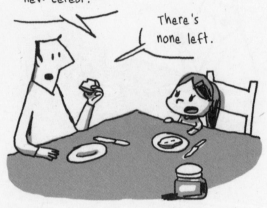

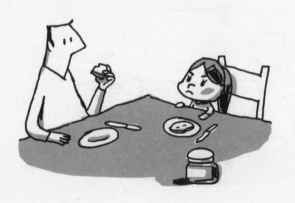

It's true! You and your brother
finished it all yesterday morning.

Don't you remember?

uh...

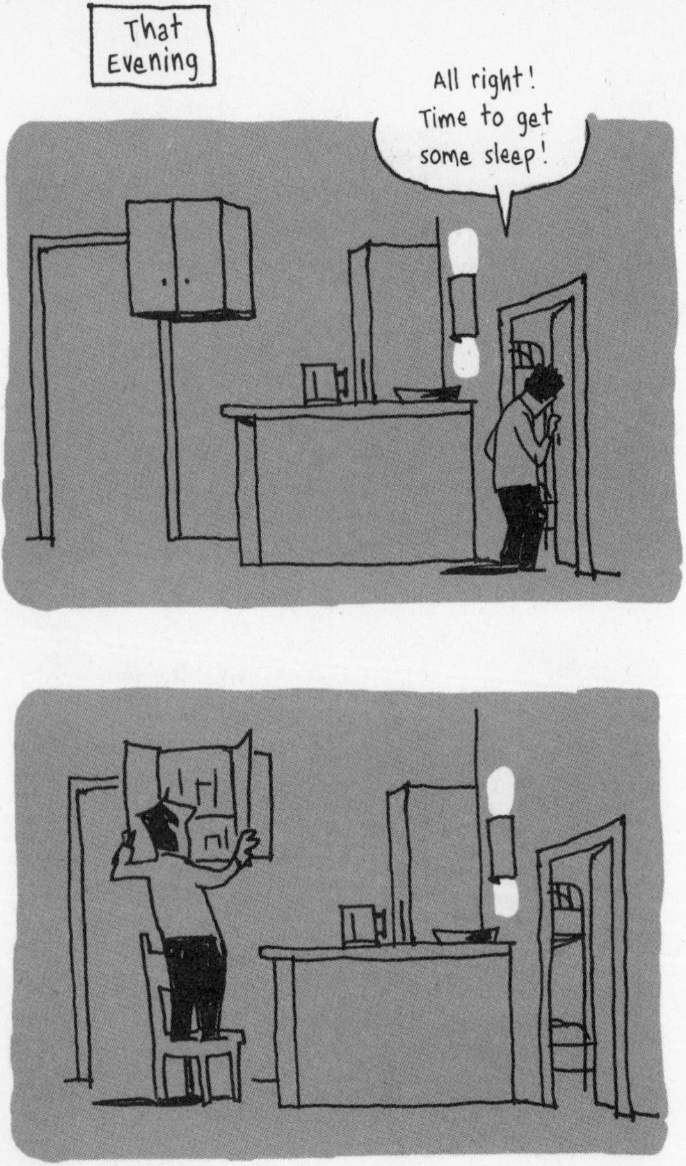
That Evening
All right! Time to get some sleep!

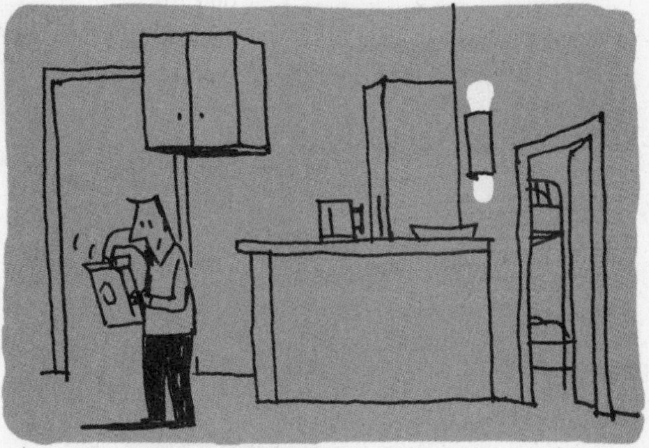

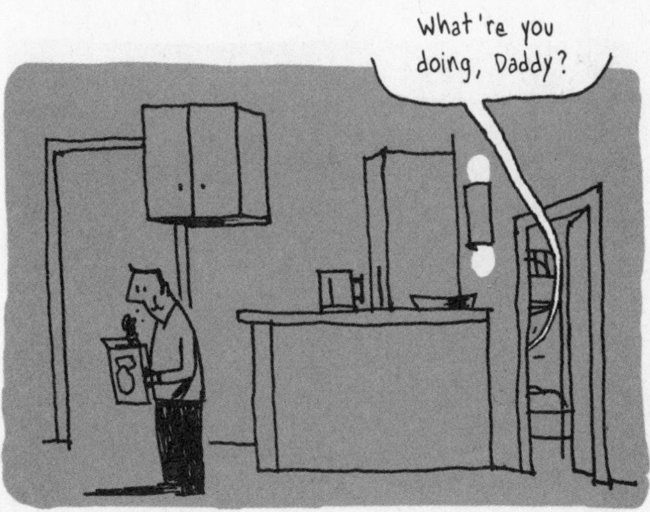
What're you doing, Daddy?

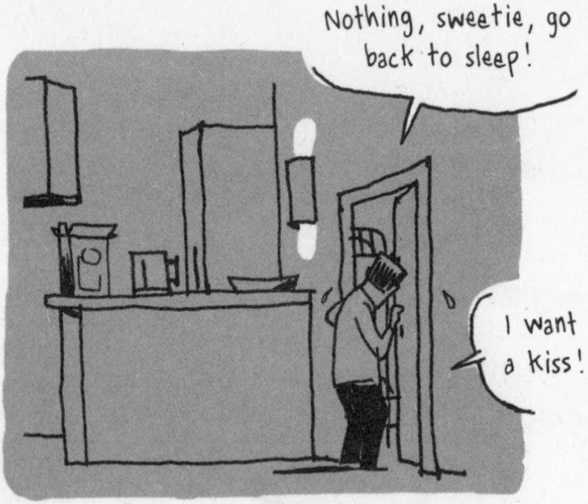
Nothing, sweetie, go back to sleep!
I want a kiss!

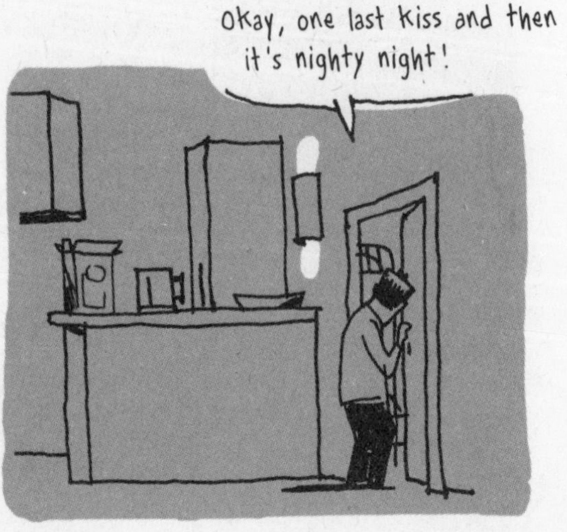
Okay, one last kiss and then it's nighty night!

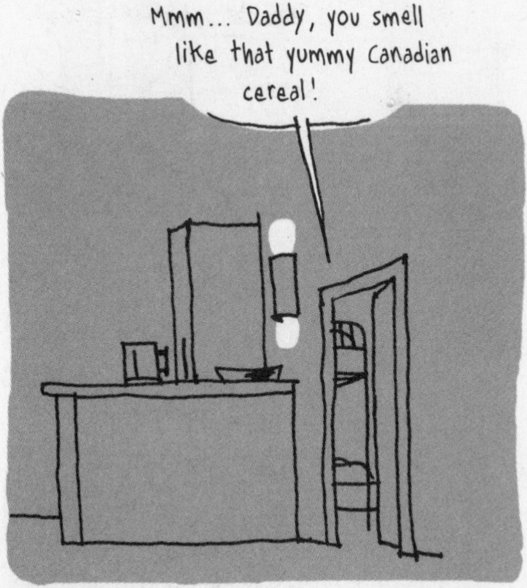
Mmm... Daddy, you smell like that yummy Canadian cereal!

DELISLE
2012

-The Handyman

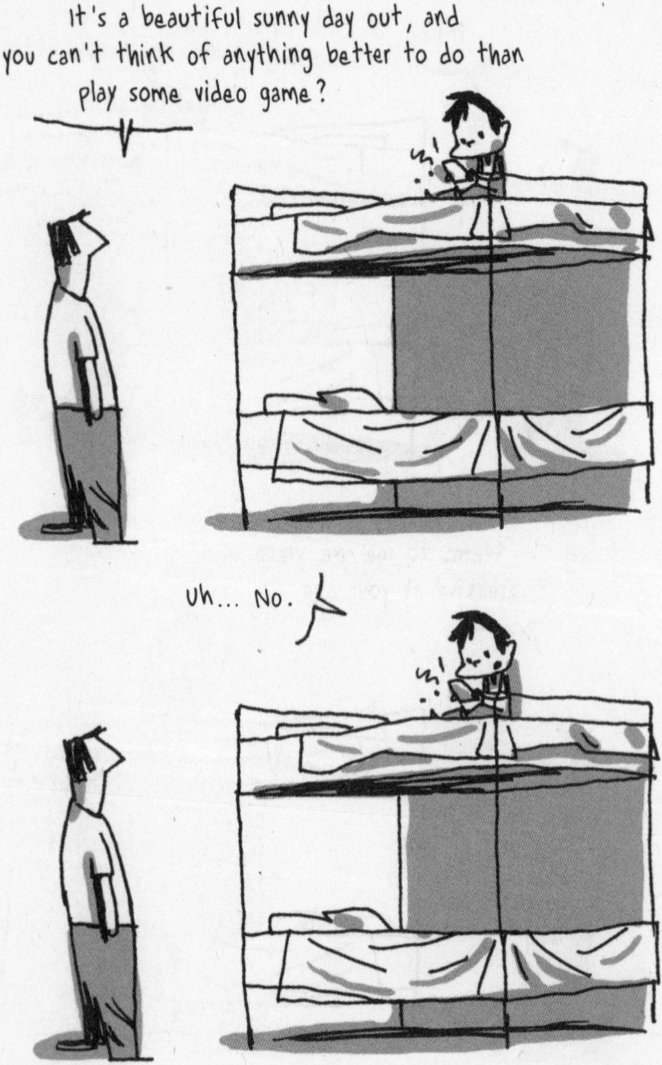
It's a beautiful sunny day out, and you can't think of anything better to do than play some video game?
Uh... No.

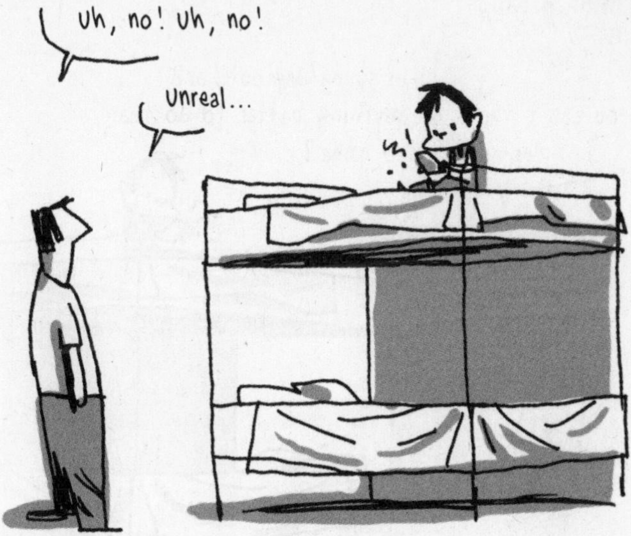
Uh, no! Uh, no!
Unreal...

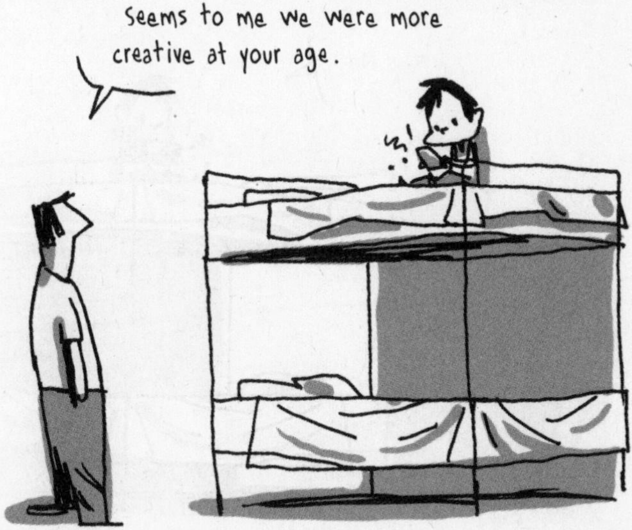
Seems to me we were more creative at your age.

We set traps, we souped up our
bicycles. I put a banana seat on mine and a big
old fork on the front wheel.

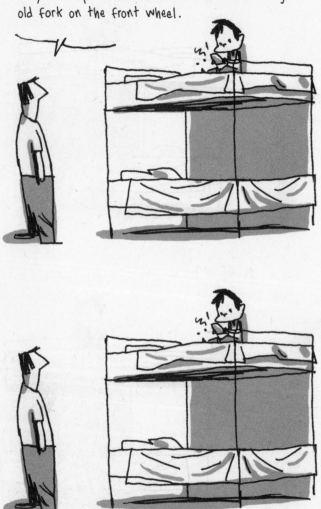

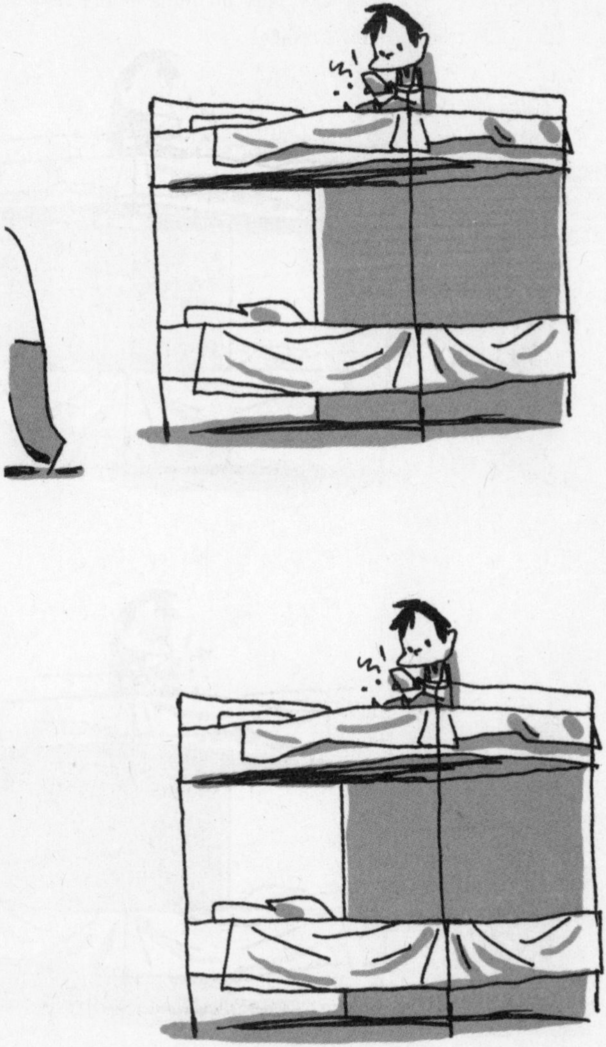

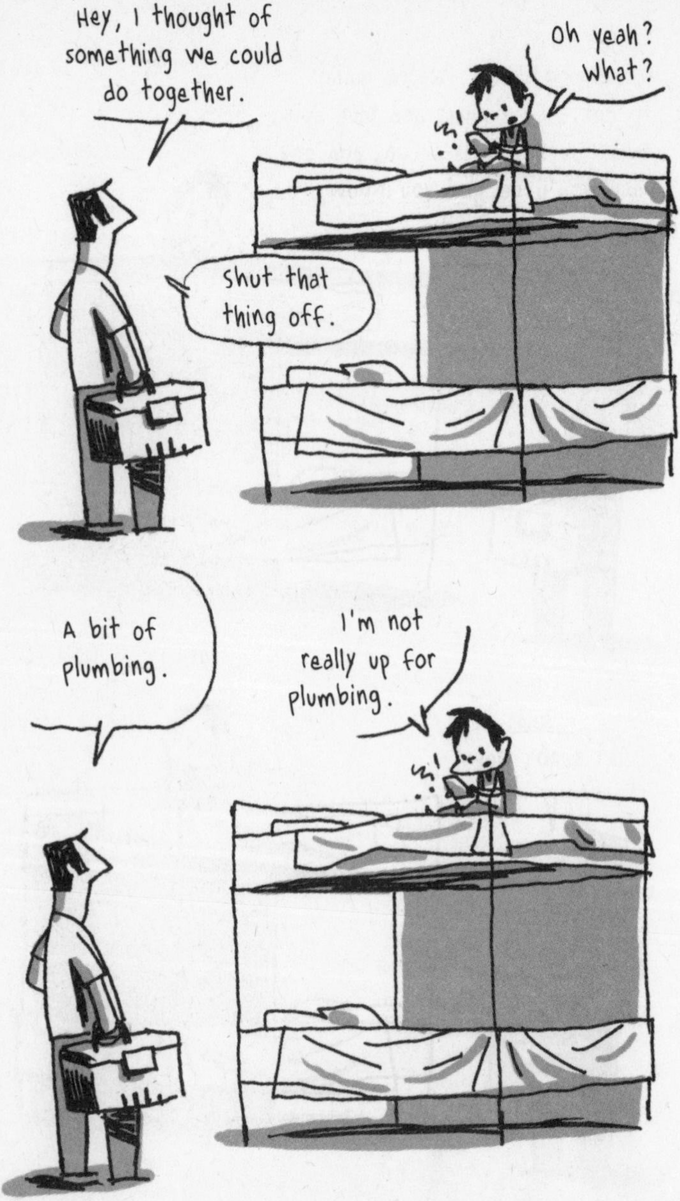
Hey, I thought of something we could do together.
Oh yeah? What?
Shut that thing off.
A bit of plumbing.
I'm not really up for plumbing.

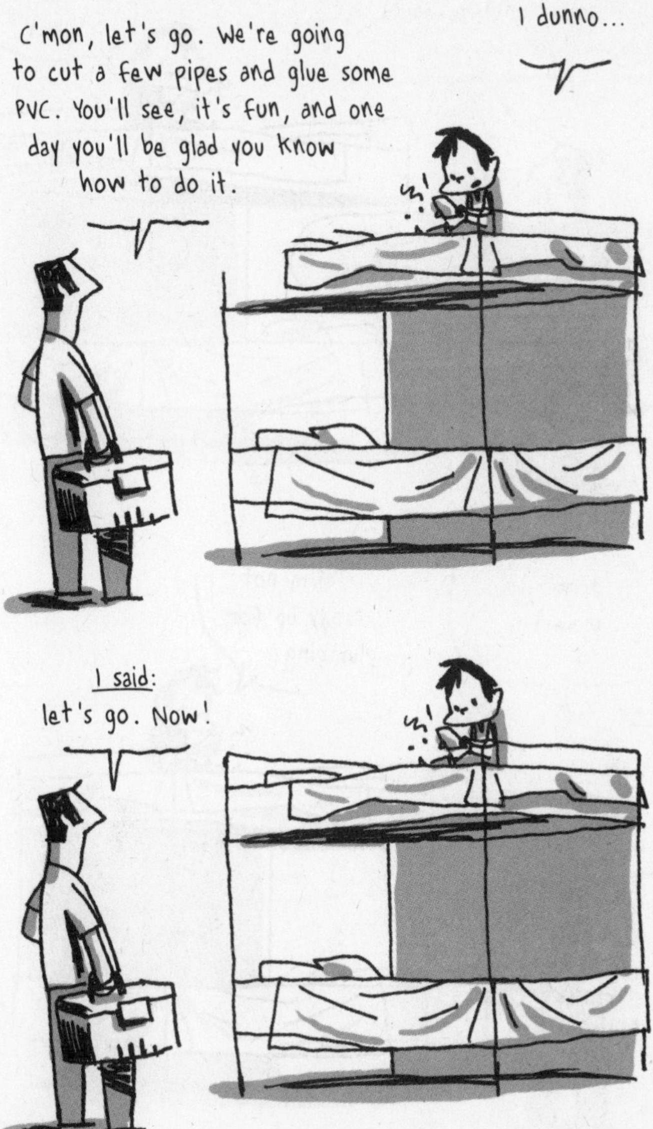
C'mon, let's go. We're going to cut a few pipes and glue some PVC. You'll see, it's fun, and one day you'll be glad you know how to do it.
I dunno...
I said:
let's go. Now!

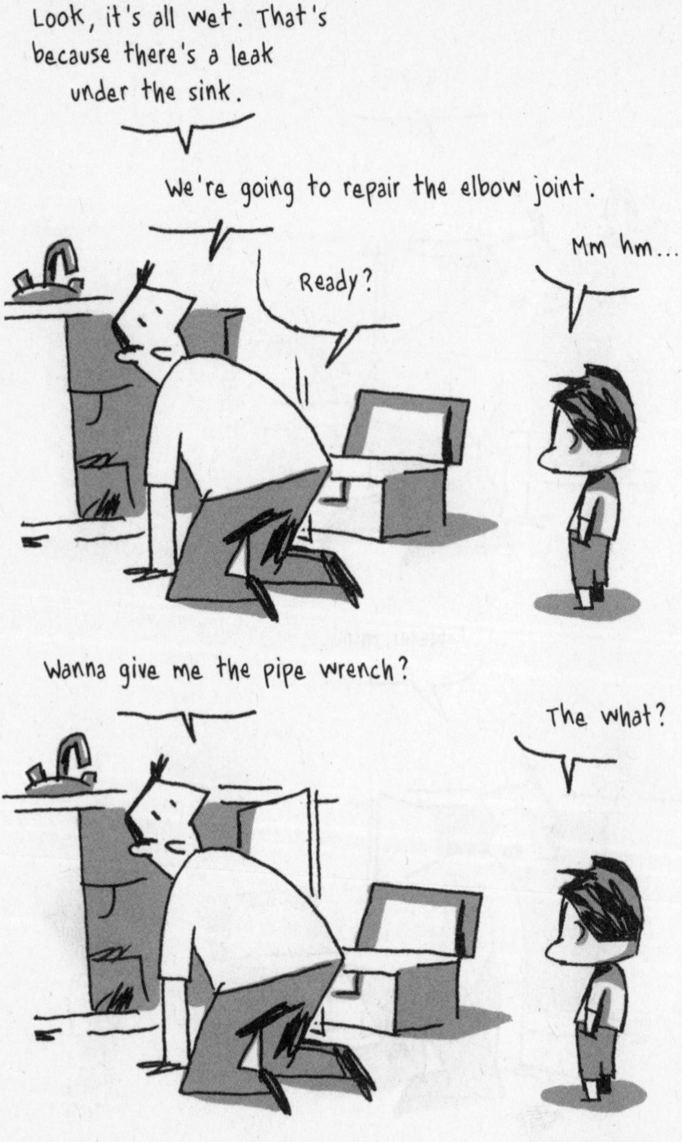
Look, it's all wet. That's because there's a leak under the sink.
We're going to repair the elbow joint.
Ready?
Mm hm...
Wanna give me the pipe wrench?
The what?

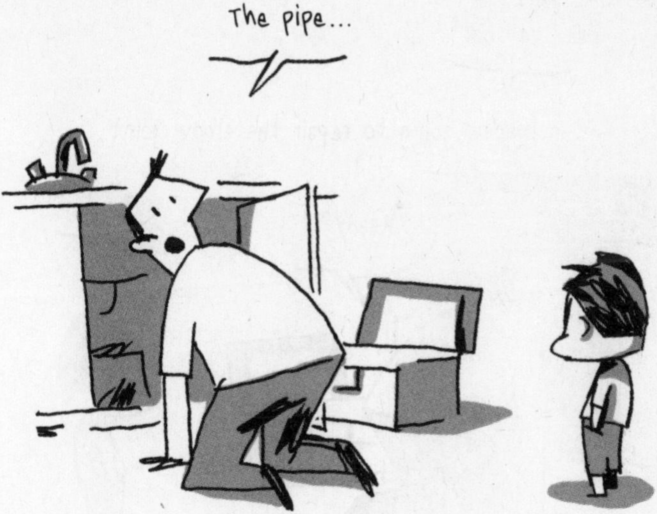
The pipe...

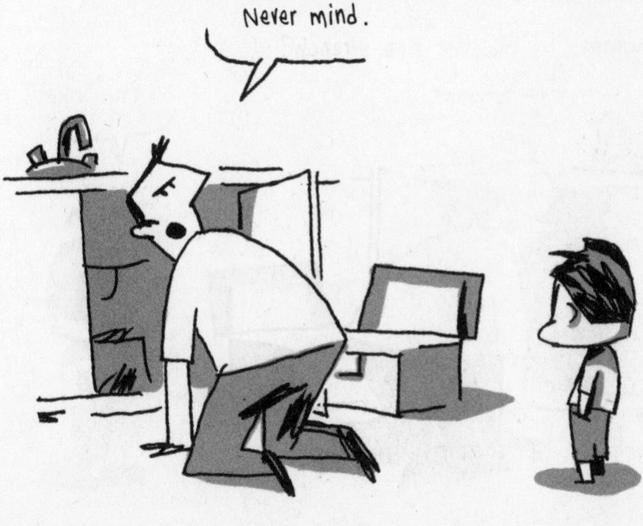
Never mind.

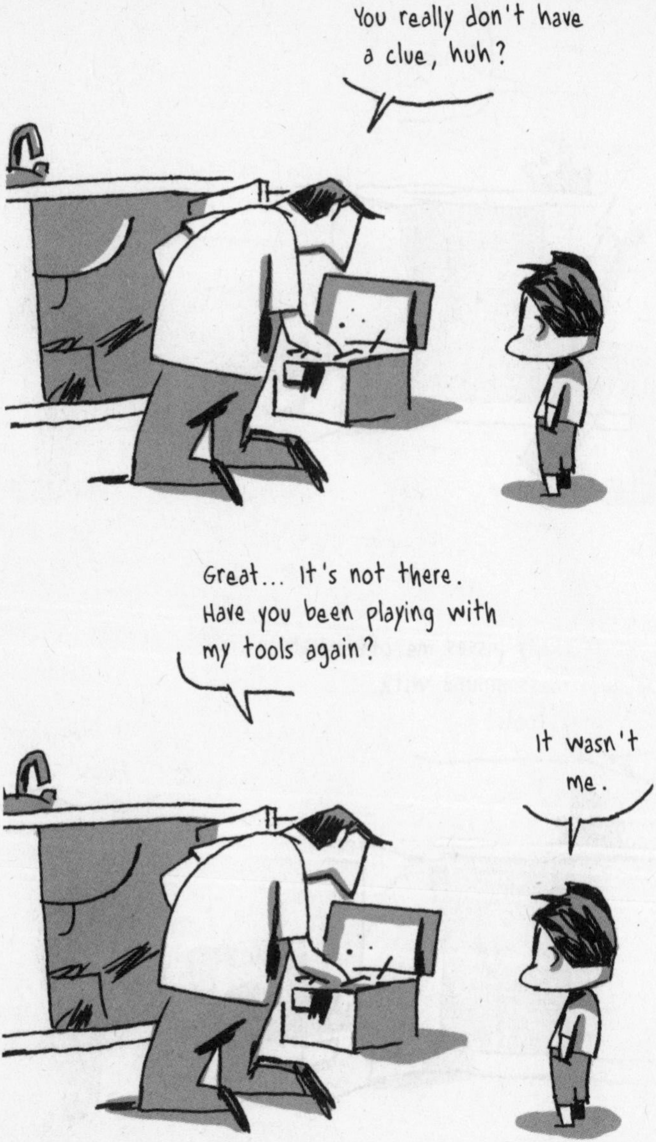
You really don't have a clue, huh?
Great... It's not there. Have you been playing with my tools again?
It wasn't me.

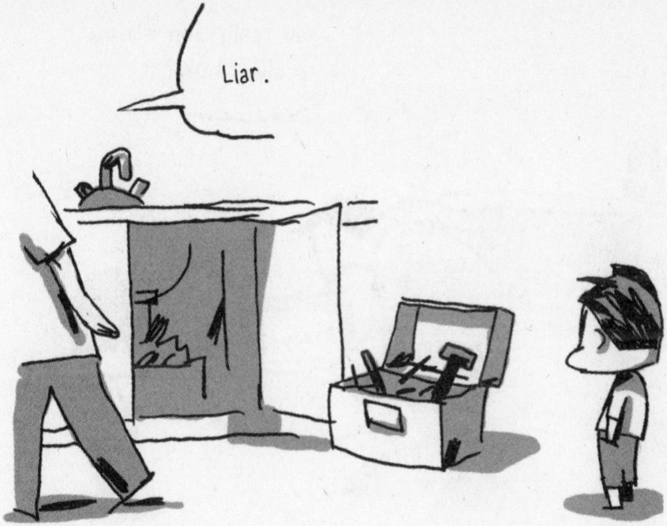
Liar.

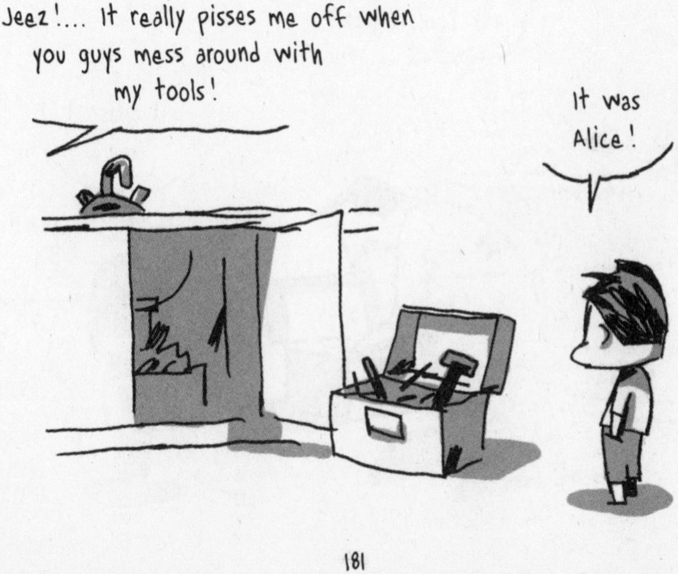
Jeez!.... It really pisses me off when you guys mess around with my tools!
It was Alice!

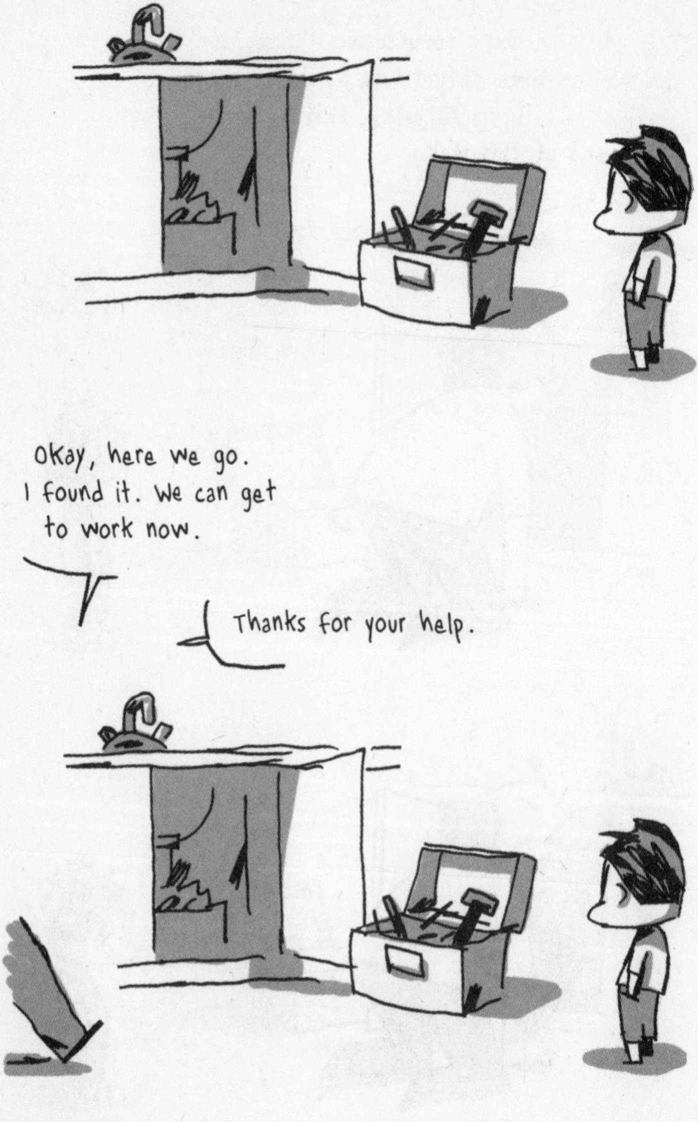
Okay, here we go. I found it. We can get to work now.
Thanks for your help.

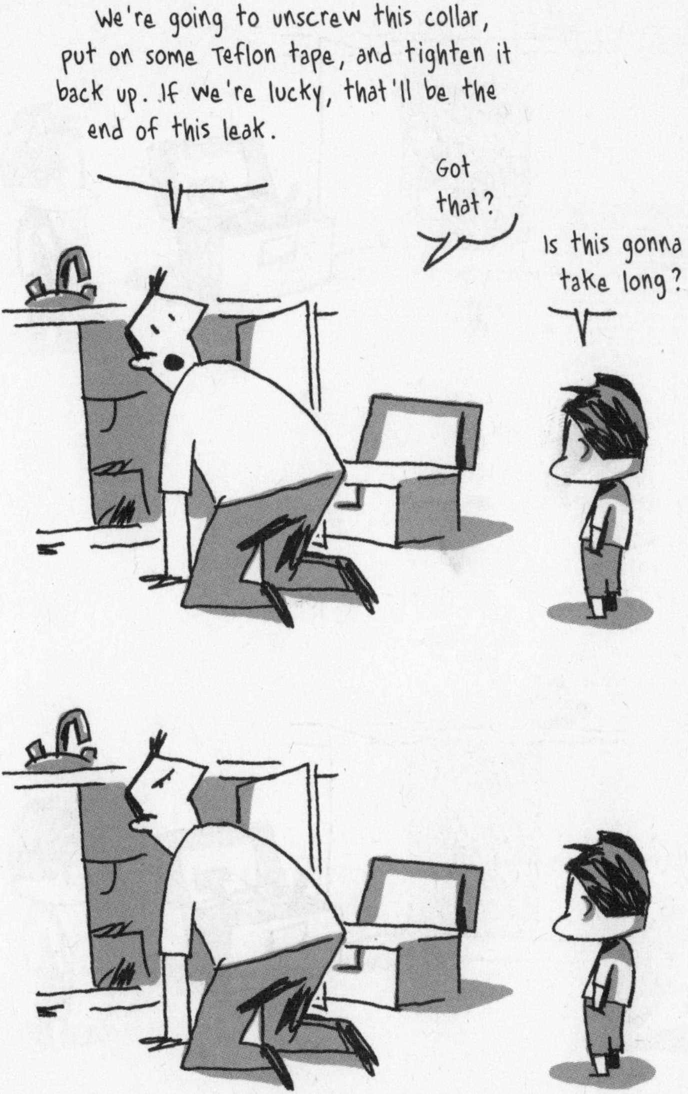
We're going to unscrew this collar, put on some Teflon tape, and tighten it back up. If we're lucky, that'll be the end of this leak.
Got that?
Is this gonna take long?

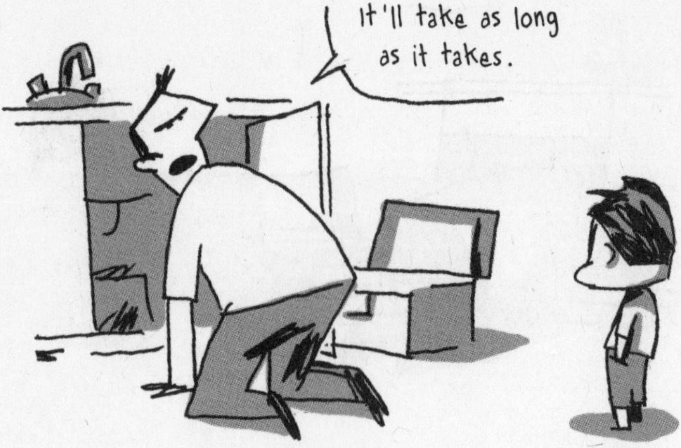
It'll take as long as it takes.

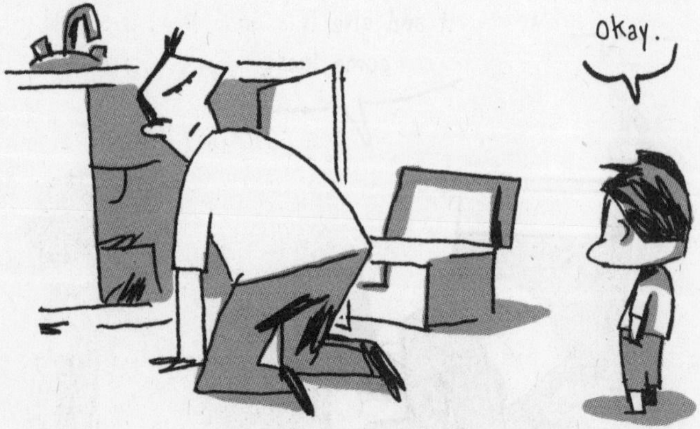
Okay.

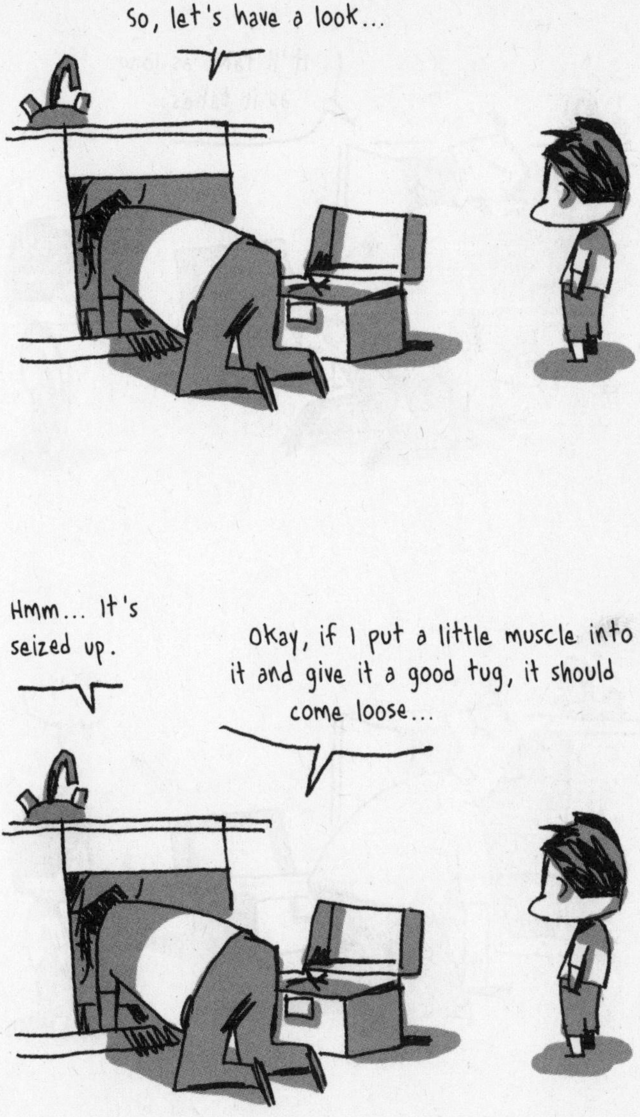
So, let's have a look...
Hmm... It's seized up.
Okay, if I put a little muscle into it and give it a good tug, it should come loose...

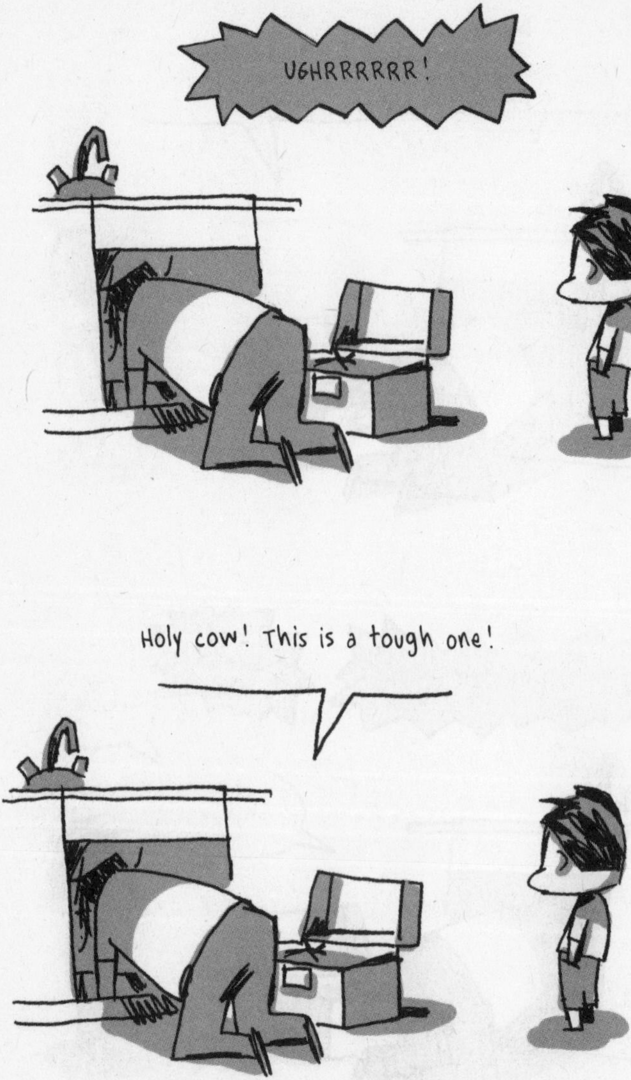
UGHRRRRRR!
Holy cow! This is a tough one!

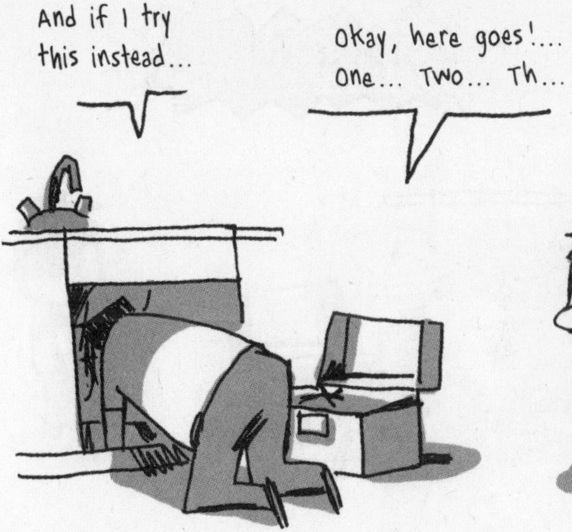
And if I try this instead...
Okay, here goes!.... One... Two... Th...

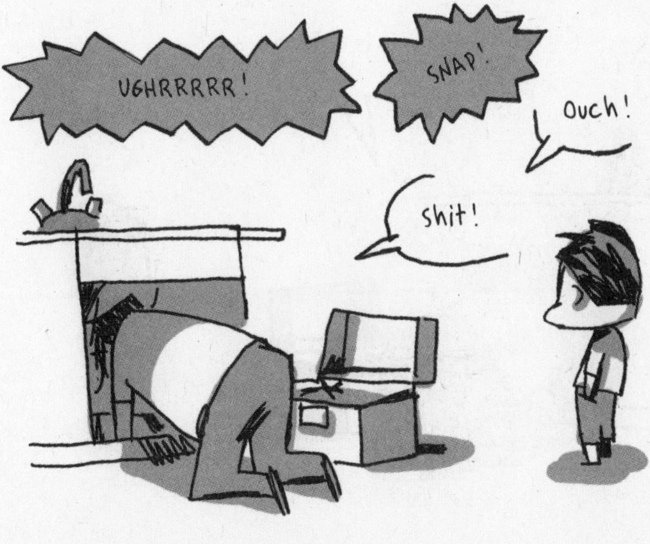
UGHRRRRR!
SNAP!
Ouch!
Shit!

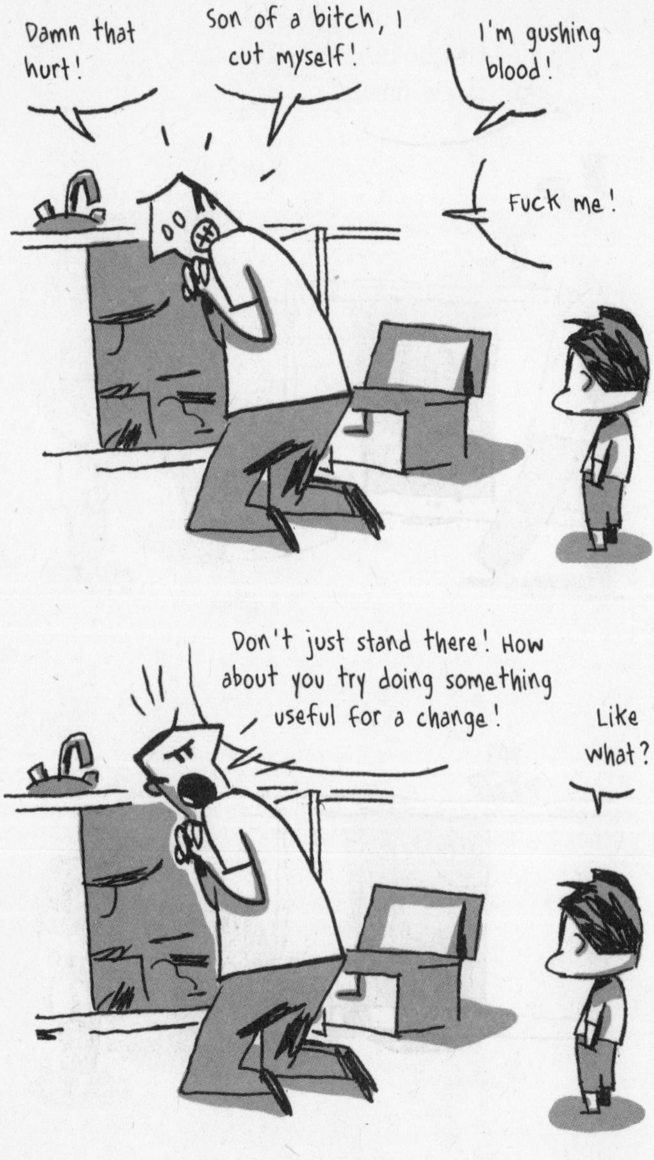
Damn that hurt!
Son of a bitch, I cut myself!
I'm gushing blood!
Fuck me!
Don't just stand there! How about you try doing something useful for a change!
Like what?

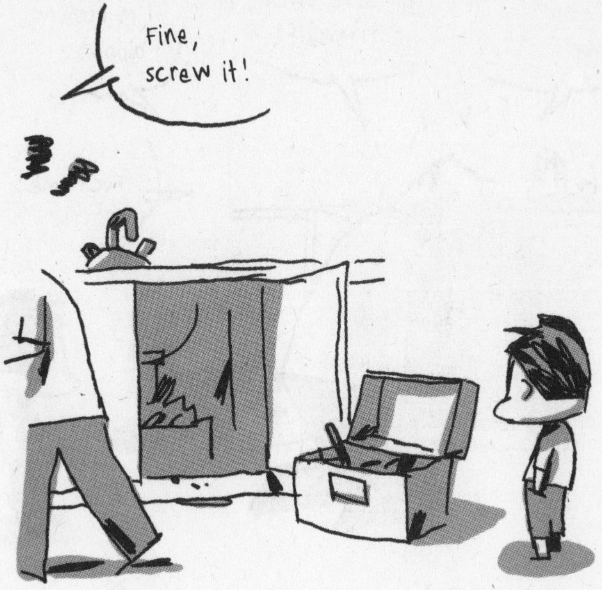
Fine,
screw it!

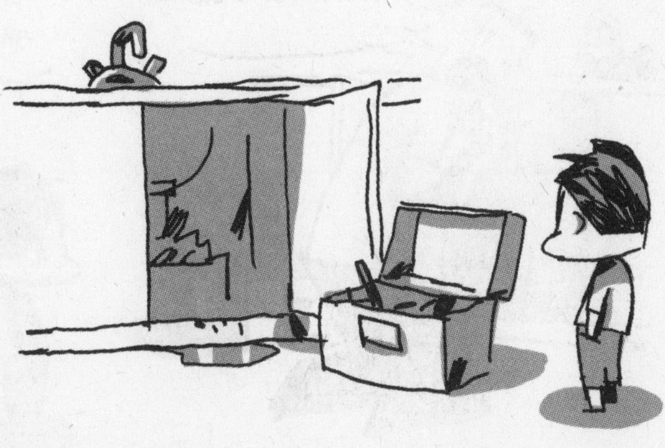

Dad!

Hey, Dad!

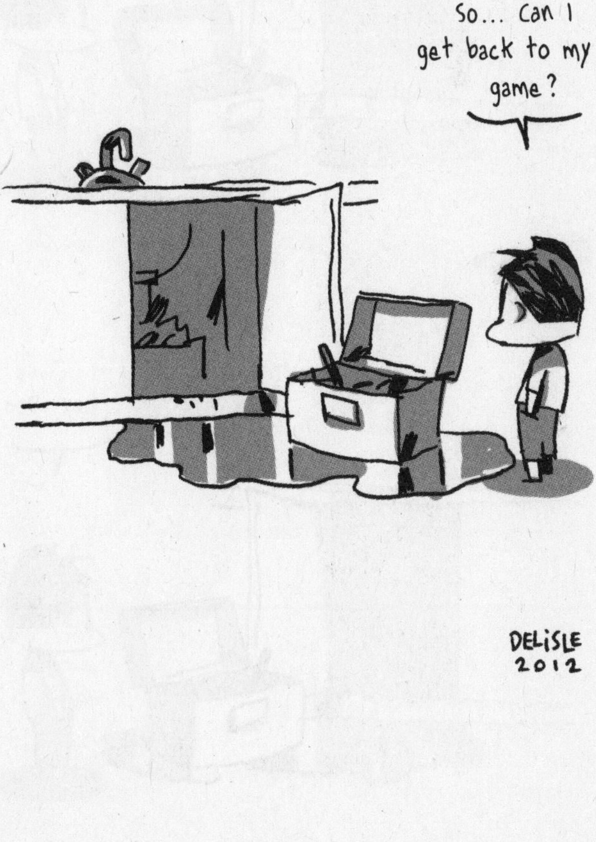
So... can I get back to my game?
DELISLE 2012